MYSTERIES IN THE DARK

VOLUME 1

STEVE STOCKTON

FREE REIGN
Publishing

CONTENTS

INTRODUCTION

Welcome friends,

In the chilling pages of *Mysteries in the Dark*, I delve into a spine-tingling collection of true stories, each more terrifying than the last. Drawing from firsthand accounts provided by witnesses themselves, this gripping anthology unearths encounters with creatures and entities that lurk within the shadows of the unknown.

Prepare to be captivated as I lead you on a journey into the heart of darkness, where the line between reality and the supernatural blurs. From deep within remote forests to dimly lit city streets, this book reveals the harrowing experiences of those who have crossed paths with the most enigmatic and fearsome beings to walk the earth.

Step into the realms of mystery and dread as witnesses recount their bone-chilling encounters with the elusive and towering figures known as Bigfoot and Sasquatch, whose existence has puzzled and intrigued humanity for generations. Discover the heart-pounding tales of those who have come face to face with the eerie and unsettling Black-Eyed Children, leaving their souls forever marked by the haunting experience.

But it doesn't end there. *Mysteries in the Dark* dares to explore even darker territories, delving into the realms of demons, malevolent spirits, and skinwalkers, entities that are the stuff of nightmares, and whose existence challenges our understanding of the natural world.

With each story more unsettling than the last, these encounters are not merely fleeting glimpses of the unknown but are experiences that have left deep imprints on the witnesses' minds, forever altering their perception of reality.

Mysteries in the Dark is not for the faint of heart, for within its pages lies a treasure trove of spine-chilling narratives that will haunt readers long after the last page is turned. Whether you are a skeptic or a firm believer in the supernatural, this gripping anthology will leave you questioning the boundaries of what lies beyond the veil of darkness and the terrifying creatures that call it home.

Are you ready to confront the inexplicable and journey into the world of the unexplained? Dare to tread into the shadows, for the mysteries that await are beyond imagination.

Steve Stockton

ONE

ENCOUNTER FROM THE DEEP

I HAD my terrifying encounter when I was out doing the most mundane of things. I was looking for my daughter's lost cat. Really the cat was a family pet, but she was a house cat and she somehow got let out that day. My daughter was eleven years old and devastated and my wife and I were worried that something would happen to her out there because we lived in a home that was surrounded by some very dense woods with some very scary and large predatory animals. My wife and I recognized the urgency to get the cat back home as soon and as quickly as possible so that night after dinner I grabbed a flashlight and headed out into the yard to look for her. I knew she had to have been in the woods somewhere but just in case my wife and daughter drove into town to hang some flyers they had made. I was praying I found the cat alive and well before it was too late, but I wasn't sure what the odds were of that happening. I called out for the cat but didn't see her anywhere and decided to go into the woods and look around too. I shined the flashlight all around, but she didn't seem to be anywhere in sight. I wasn't about to give up and thought I would stay out there all night long if necessary, so my daughter didn't have to go through the trauma of losing her beloved pet that had been with the family since before she was even born. I was concerned about the fact that there were also some underground tunnels in the woods behind my house and though I had never had the nerve to go in them, I knew a cat wouldn't be as smart as I had been. I was scared to go down in them, but it got to where I knew I had to at least check. No one was supposed to go anywhere near the tunnels and there were signs posted literally everywhere that no one is allowed to enter. There was metal grating, like a prison cell or something, at the edge of the tunnel so that no human beings could enter but someone else had already cut through it, so it was easy for me to get inside. I am a slim man and only five foot eight so the tunnel was large enough that I could stand up easily and walk normally. I had worn work boots which was good because the floor was a little damp and there was some water. The whole place smelled so incredibly foul and horrible that it took everything I had not to vomit or turn around and leave within seconds of getting inside of there.

I saw dead rats all along the walls in the place and thought that was bizarre. I only saw them from a distance and only through the beam of my small flashlight, but they somehow didn't look natural to me. The way they were all piled on top of one another, and I had a bad feeling from the moment I had gotten all the way down into the depths of this thing. I also didn't hear or see any live rats anywhere and though I was relieved, it stood to reason by all the dead ones that there should have been live ones there too, right? That's what I thought at the time, anyway. It was eerily quiet down there, but I called out to the cat anyway. My voice loudly echoed all throughout the tunnel and I was startled by it the first time it echoed back to me. It made me jump. I had been walking through the tunnel for a good fifteen minutes when it looked like something had run or crawled across the ground in front of me. I saw it as quick as a flash, but I knew it was there because it interrupted the beam of my light. Plus, I heard something up ahead of me scuttling through the water on the ground. I jumped back and almost dropped the flashlight. I called out, asking who was there, but I didn't receive a response. I decided that if I didn't find the cat in the next ten minutes that I was going to turn around and just leave. I often wish I had just left right then or that I had never entered that tunnel to begin with. The thing that ran in front of me on the ground, or crawled- I still wasn't sure which it had done, had been about ten feet in front of me. Once I reached that spot, I shined the flashlight all around and even behind me but didn't see anything. I didn't hear anything except the sound of my own breathing and heartbeat, and that's also when I noticed there was nowhere for anything to have gone. The tunnel was just that, a tunnel, and the only way for anyone or anything to go at that point was back the way I had come or forward, the way I was heading then. I didn't know what to think but I tried to put it out of my head completely.

I walked for another few minutes and started to hear what sounded like scratching sounds all along the walls and up above me. I was too scared to look and decided right then to turn around and get out of there. I didn't want to run because I was afraid some animal was down there that was watching me somehow and I figured if I ran that would be all whatever it was needed to chase me down and do God knows what to me. Then, right after I turned around, I heard a strange sound that I can only describe as, "Yak Yak Yak." I jumped because of course it echoed loudly throughout the entire tunnel. I didn't turn around to look even though that's where it had come from, and I just picked up the pace a little bit so that I could get out of there much faster. Eventually I had come to the end of the tunnel where I had originally gone in. I got out of there faster than I had ever moved before in my life. Something had been following me and I knew that because of the sound its feet made in the small puddle of water that was all along the floor of the tunnel. Whatever it was, it had been large, and it wasn't a cat, a rat, a bat, or any other small and somewhat harmless creature that I could easily win in a fight against. I got about five feet away from the tunnel and turned around. I shined my flashlight on the entrance that I had just come out of, but I didn't see anything. I didn't hear anything either and anyone who knows what the wilderness sounds like at night knows that's a troubling thing all on its own. It means there's a large predator in the area that the other animals see, sense, or otherwise know is there and they've all gone and hidden out of fear. It wasn't me, either I wasn't the large predator because animals don't stop running around on the forest floor, owls don't stop hooting and insects don't stop chirping because there's a human being among them. I shined the flashlight everywhere but still didn't see anything. I briefly started walking in the direction of my house but then I thought of my heartbroken daughter and how she would react or even how she would have gotten through the night if her beloved pet and friend wasn't home with her. I had to keep going. I had to brave whatever was out there until I found the cat or at the very least did everything in my power to try to find her. I told myself I was being silly and that I needed to get back out there for my daughter. So, I turned around and started walking deeper into the woods.

Right when I was in the general vicinity of the swamp, I started to hear that same "yak yak yak" sound echoing all around me. It was very loud and much more noticeable because nothing else out there was making any noise. I saw something once again run through the beam of the flashlight, but I knew at that time that it was the cat. I had found the cat! I called out to her, but she kept right on running deeper into the woods and towards the tunnel and the swamp. I was agitated at that point but had to keep on going. I heard her meow and got excited. I walked quickly, I couldn't run because I couldn't see too far in front of me, but I knew I was going in the right direction when I heard her meowing again. Then, suddenly, I heard her let out an extremely loud sound that told me she was being hurt. I stopped for a second to listen and heard her hissing. I had grown up around cats and knew a lot about them and from what I was hearing, something had gotten a hold of the cat or scared her. Either way, I had to go and get her. I was terrified and it was like going against my own instincts the whole time just to keep walking in the direction I knew the cat was. I called out for her, and she meowed again but then hissed again as well. Finally, I saw her standing on some rocks that were right in front of the swamp area. The large rocks were almost like a barrier between the rest of the forest and the swamp, and they went all around it. I called her but she was distracted by whatever she was looking at in the swamp. Her back was raised, and all her hair was standing on end. She was growling and mewling too. She obviously felt threatened and was about to attack something. I heard the yak sounds again as I climbed onto the rocks next to the cat and scooped her up with my one hand while still holding the flashlight with my other. She screeched at me and tried to claw my face which was very much out of character but once I spoke to her in a soothing voice and started petting her, she calmed down and cuddled into me. She was still looking at the swamp behind us. I had to see what was there. A part of me was hoping there was some very ordinary explanation, and I could then make my way out of there without having to be nervous about what could have been following me. I turned and shined my flashlight onto the swampy water. That's when I saw the most hideous and terrifying creature one's mind could even imagine.

It had a face that looked somewhat like a frog and the same bulging eyes. It stood on two legs though and had those fan things on the sides of its face that most lizards have. Its skin was green, but it was several different shades of the color. It had webbed hands and feet and stood at around five feet tall. It had red or orange eyes and it just seemed evil to me even though it was merely standing there and looking at me. It opened its mouth and hissed at me and then I saw its sharp, razor fanged teeth. It got down on all fours and laughed itself onto the rocks that the cat and I had just been on. It flicked out its tongue, but it didn't reach us, though it was horrifyingly long and almost coming close to touching my leg. The cat started going crazy again and once the creature noticed the cat trying to get out of my arms and that she was growling and hissing again, it opened its mouth and in that same guttural and deep voice it made the yak sounds. I turned and ran and heard the creature land behind me. It must have hopped off the rocks and onto the ground. I thought it would chase us, but it didn't, and I knew that quickly because as fast as I was running out of there, I had covered a good amount of ground and heard the sounds it made but from a distance. It must have just been trying to scare me out of there. I made it home with the cat and my daughter and wife were so happy and excited. Of course, I never told them a thing about it, but I was more mindful of allowing my daughter to go into the woods to play and stopped letting her do that for the most part. I never explained myself as to why my mind had changed so suddenly but no one really questioned it and she just stayed out of the woods and wasn't allowed to ever be in them at night or alone ever again. Not that she was prone to nighttime excursions through the forest in the first place. I think I disturbed the creature when I was in the tunnel, and it had followed me out into the forest. I think it's what ate the rats and had its sights set on my cat. If I hadn't showed up when I did, I know I got tremendously lucky, it probably would have flicked out its tongue or something and eaten my cat too. I have never been the same because now I know there are creatures and things out there, in this world, that we as human beings have no concept of and some of those things can be deadly.

TWO

A WEREWOLF?

MY ENCOUNTER HAPPENED in Texas in the early 2000s. I was twenty-five years old and just decided to randomly go on a weekend camping trip with some of my friends. None of us had anything to do that weekend and one of them suggested going into the woods for the weekend to hang out and have some fun. We would hike and fish, depending on the season and the weather, and otherwise just have a good time. None of us were hunters but we had all grown up in, near and around densely wooded areas and we were all into nature. We were familiar with all the local wildlife and had never had any real problems with any of the wild animals out in the woods. It was honestly just something else to do on a weekend at the end of summer. It was myself, my best friend Kenny, and his friend Grant. We originally thought we would go camping until Grant said that his parent's cabin on the lake was empty for the weekend and he called and asked if we could go there and hang out. The cabin was a nice one and it was in this little community around the lake, but the entire place looked like it had been airlifted from somewhere and dropped directly in the middle of the forest. The people who lived there had vehicles, but they hardly ever used them and instead rode around on ATVs because aside from the one road leading in and out, the whole place was just a bunch of woods and trails. The lake wasn't that big, but it was clean and had a filter in it. Once the cabin was mentioned we were even more excited, and we couldn't wait to get out there and just get away from it all for the whole weekend. I had grown up with those guys, so I knew their parents well and they treated me and Kenny like another son. It was shaping up to be a really great time and before we knew it was Friday afternoon and time to hit the road.

We all met at Kenny's house after work on Friday and decided to just take his truck out there. It was located about two hours away from his parents' main house and all we had to do was stop at the store and pick up some groceries. None of us really drank and we certainly didn't do drugs. We didn't pick up any alcohol because we knew if it came down to it his dad always had beer in the fridge in the basement and they had a full bar down there too. We mainly liked to spend a lot of time in the woods doing things, so we didn't often drink at all while we were there except when his parents were throwing a party or something. We got there at twilight which was my favorite time at the lake. The way the setting sun twinkled off the water just made me feel so at peace. I rented a small apartment in an over-crowded area of a big city, so the lake was a peaceful place for me. Grant's parent's neighbors were all nice too, though we noticed when we drove in that most of them didn't look like they were home. The lake was man made so it was in the shape of a circle and there were about twelve houses that all surrounded it in the development, with the lake being in everyone's backyard. That's just to explain the setup a little bit better. It didn't matter to us if anyone was home or not and we quickly went to work bringing our stuff in from the truck, unpacking, setting up in our individual rooms and then cooking some food on the grill. We were eating on the back deck when we heard what sounded like someone screaming inside of the woods. That normally wouldn't have been too unusual because kids hang out in the woods all the time and some of them party and drink or get high. However, the development was private, and it was concerning that maybe it was one of the neighbors or something so we listened more closely to see if we could discern what it was. It happened again almost immediately and realized it sounded like an animal was in pain and it wasn't a human being. We all kind of forgot about it and once it was fully dark and we were all done eating, we decided to watch a movie. We watched a horror movie, of course, and after that I wanted to go get some fresh air in the forest. The lake was so small I could've walked around it in like ten minutes, so I decided to take one of the ATVs out onto the trails and just ride around for a little while. It wasn't that late, only like nine pm, and so I thought the guys would be down to go with me. Both said they were too tired though and so I was on my own. I needed to let loose and had a lot of stress happening in my life at that time, so I just jumped on the ATV and went for it. I told them I would be back in about an hour or maybe less. We all said goodbye and off I went.

It didn't take very long, once I got into the woods, for me to get a very strange feeling. I never felt uncomfortable out there but the feeling I had at that moment was something different altogether. It was like I knew that I wasn't alone, despite there being no one and nothing else around me for as far as the eye could see. Now, don't get me wrong, there were the usual nighttime and nocturnal forest creatures and they all seemed to be doing what they always did and making all the usual noises but the feelings not only of being intensely watched but also of extreme dread that overtook me so suddenly was very overwhelming. I had to stop the ATV because my body was trembling, and my hands were sweating so badly, and it all seemed like it was happening for no good or rational reason. This whole experience has taught me to pay close attention to my body because if I had been paying attention that night, I might've taken the hint that something was very wrong, and I needed to get the hell out of there as quickly as possible. But I didn't take the hints my body and mind were giving me and after sitting for a few minutes and taking a few deep breaths, I went on my way again. I stopped after about twenty minutes and got off the ATV. I sat down on a log underneath an odd-looking tree and just prayed. I didn't want my friends to know that I had recently become somewhat religious because even at twenty-five years old I was afraid of what they would think. I was foolish and in fact when they found out they supported me a lot. I was praying when I started to hear that screaming noise again that we had all heard while we were out there on the deck having dinner. It sounded a lot lower though, like they wouldn't be hearing it back at the house if they were outside like we had earlier, and it also sounded weaker somehow. I became convinced an animal had somehow gotten hurt and was dying out there, some-where right near where I was. I took my flashlight and looked around on the ground a little bit, but I didn't find anything and after a few minutes the noises stopped again. It sounded like a suffering deer, once I really heard it up close and gave it a little more thought, but it didn't make sense to me that we would've heard a deer from such a distance. I tried to shrug it off and push it all down, along with the uncomfortable feelings of dread and terror that were once again resurfacing inside of me as I stood there. I decided to get back on the ATV and get the hell out of there. Something strange and messed up was happening or it was about to, and I didn't want any part of whatever it was.

I don't know how I knew that, but I somehow just did, and I was sure of it. As soon as I sat down on the quad and turned the engine over, the headlights went on. Before I could move at all, something came walking out of the forest and stepped right in front of me. It took me blinking several times to make sure that I really was seeing what I was seeing. I was in shock and my heart immediately dropped down into my feet and started to skip multiple beats. I had never and have never experi-enced terror like I was in those moments when that thing stepped right out in front of me. At first it was like I wasn't even there but then, it turned to look at me. It was about seven feet tall and standing on two legs. It walked like a human being but there was nothing at all that was human about this thing. It wasn't like you see in the movies where the werewolf looks somewhat human and somewhat canine or wolf-like. This thing looked like it was all canine and just happened to walk like a human. Its legs were thin but muscular and the arms were weird. They were very thin and spindly, not too muscular at all, and reminded me of a Tyrannosaurus Rex with how short they were. They didn't even hang down past the thing's hips. It was about thirty feet in front of me and it wasn't registering right away. When it looked at me, I could see that it had red stuff all over its mouth, or its muzzle, and its fur was a purplish gray color with patches of white all over the place. It was very obviously a female because it had breasts like a female has and the lower region also looked female. It was so strange because those things about it, those features if you will, were also very human-like in appearance and not what you would imagine a dog, wolf or mostly any other animal would have in those places on its body. Its eyes were bright yellowish-orange and they seemed to be glowing. I didn't know though if it was because the headlights were shining on it or if that's how they just looked. There was something else about the eyes as well that really stood out to me. They were binocular, like a fish's eyes and they seemed to stick out of the head a little bit. The creature just looked at me, it showed its fangs and growled at me but lowly, like a dog does when it's trying to scare someone into submission. I didn't react because I was afraid that any move, I made would possibly startle it or be viewed as an act of aggression and I didn't want it to attack me. I knew if it would have attacked me, it would have ripped me apart. I'm very sure of that fact too.

I guess it realized I wasn't a threat and based on the blood hanging off its chin and all over its mouth, coupled with the fact that I had been hearing a deer suffering, slowly dying and in pain somewhere in the area just moments earlier, it must've already eaten and wasn't hungry anymore because after staring at me for what seemed like an eternity but was probably only a minute or two, it simply walked off into the woods as casually and as slowly as it had originally wandered out of them. I breathed a sigh of relief and once it had been fully out of my sight for a good five minutes, I hauled ass out of there and didn't bother looking back. I immediately told Kenny and Grant what I had seen, and they believed me. It wasn't because they had ever seen something like that before, but because they could tell by my demeanor that I wasn't lying. I wasn't really known for my ability to lie well or make up wild stories to try and scare my friends. I was a panicked and nervous wreck by the time I was back to the cabin and telling them what happened. We never saw the creature again, but it has made me so much more mindful and aware of my surroundings when I'm out in the woods and I never go out into the woods for any reason unarmed.

THREE

DOGMAN ENCOUNTER

WHEN I WAS A LITTLE GIRL, I used to love to go on picnics down by the lake behind our house. It wasn't on our property and was located behind and somewhat within some woods that surrounded our house. The lake was surrounded by woods too and had at one time been a public recreation area. It belonged at the time I would go by it to the residents of an upscale community located within the confines of a security gate. They had to walk through the woods to get to it as well and it was supposed to be exclusive to those residents, but no one had ever said anything to me and it was often the case that I would meet other little kids there who lived in the community and we would play while their parents swam, barbequed or otherwise just relaxed in the sun. It was an early spring that year, at least as far as the weather was concerned and I couldn't wait to go and have my first picnic of the season down by the lake. I was only about ten years old, and we didn't own a phone in our house so there was no way for me to contact the kids I met so that we could meet up. Sometimes we would make plans for the following day but once the warm weather was gone, I didn't see any of them anymore because even though they lived somewhat close to me, they were from the upscale private community, and they all went to private schools. I went to a public school and came from a family that was only an inch above the poverty line. It was the nineteen seventies and social distinctions like that of wealth were made back then. It's just the way things were, and no one was ever offended by it. The kids were nice to me even if their parents always gave me strange looks and acted like the food, I brought with me was tainted with dirt or something. They never wanted their kids eating anything I brought with me but would always encourage them to share with me. That has nothing to do with the encounter, not really, but I wanted to set the scene for you a little bit, nonetheless.

My father, my uncles and all their friends were avid outdoorsmen and hunters. Sometimes I would overhear them talking about their adventures in the woods and about some of the strange things that they had seen out there. They didn't go hunting in the woods behind our house of course but they did go other places in town where they were allowed to do so, during the right seasons of course, and they told some wild stories. I always chalked it up to them trying to playfully scare us or maybe to the copious amounts of beer they drank when they would all get together and tell those kinds of stories and there was one creature, they spoke about a lot. I didn't ever think much about it, and it never really frightened me because I made the distinction of how nice the woods were behind our house and how nice the lake was, and I thought there was no way any sort of horrible and terrifying creatures could be lurking around out there. I didn't realize until I was much older that the main creature, they would all discuss having seen and wanting to catch was bigfoot. They spoke about other, much scarier ones too, and that's where my encounter comes into the picture. I wasn't lucky enough to see a bigfoot and in fact saw something much more terrifying, in my opinion and especially to my ten-year-old eyes.

I made some sandwiches and packed some juice after putting my clothes on top of my swimsuit before heading out to the lake. I knew there were sometimes dangerous animals out there in the spring but the sounds of all the people usually scared or otherwise kept them away. Plus, I was taught how to handle each one, should

I happen to come across one and feel threatened. That had never happened before, and I never expected that it would. The second I stepped into the wood's things felt weird. I played in the woods even in the wintertime but never went down to the lake. The ice was too thin and unreliable to ice skate in, or so my mom said, and it wasn't like I owned a pair of ice skates or would have known what I was doing anyway. I felt like I was being watched and it was a scary feeling. I also noticed that, for a very beautiful and bright day in the springtime, it was quiet out there. I tried my best to ignore it because I was so young and the excitement of seeing my friends who I hadn't seen for several months at that point was more important to me than some weird feelings I was having. I wish I would have listened to my instincts and immediately turned around and hot out of there. I was only little though, and I wasn't patient enough to understand that the next day would be just as nice and maybe wouldn't have felt so strange and scary right from the door. I was determined to play with my friends and so I tried as best as I could to shake off the strange and scary feelings. One of the thoughts that came into my mind was that maybe the animals were smelling my food and following me through the woods or something like that.

I finally got to the lake and even that was weird because I didn't hear all the giggling and laughter like I normally would have on such a beautiful day. It may have been too chilly to swim for the adults, but it wasn't the coolest it had ever been when I had been there swimming with the other kids. I was shocked when I got there and saw that there wasn't a single other person in sight. That hadn't ever happened to me before. The place just seemed eerie, and it was still silent as far as the sounds that should have been coming out of the woods at that time of day and then with no people being there except for me, it made it all the scarier for me. I decided to sit down and set up my picnic. I wasn't allowed to swim without anyone else there with me and I figured someone would have to be coming along shortly. I sat down at one of the picnic tables and no sooner had I done so then I saw a huge bear come running out of the woods. It kept looking back and making a strange noise. I found out later that the noise I was hearing was the noise a bear makes when it's in pain or scared. It could have been both. I immediately jumped up, but I didn't move away from the table. This was all happening about fifty feet or so away from me and I didn't want to get in the way of whatever was happening with the bear and whatever else was out there, causing it to behave the way it was. It was retreating from something, something it kept looking back at to see if it was being followed. There came a point where the bear and I made eye contact, and my heart skipped a beat, but it just made the strange and pathetic noise again before limping as it ran around the lake and into the other side of the woods. I should mention here before I go on that I wore glasses as a kid, but my vision wasn't too terrible. I knew what a bear looked like so I easily put together what was going on but what happened next, I didn't immediately understand and that could be because my eyes weren't understanding what was right in front of me. Whether it be because of my vision or my brain not being able to make the right connections but either way, here it is.

Someone came running out of the woods right behind the bear and at first, because it seemed like it was running on two legs, I thought it was a human man. I just watched as it ran very quickly out of the woods, the same way the bear had come from and started going the same way too. It was only when it got down on all fours and growled very loudly that it wasn't a man at all, and I might be in some serious trouble and danger. I stood there, hoping I looked as small as I felt so that the thing maybe wouldn't see me. The thing, whatever it was I still didn't know at that point, did see me though and it stopped dead in its tracks and turned towards me as soon as it spotted me. It stood back up on its hind legs and slowly started coming closer. It got to where it was approximately twenty feet away from me and with glasses or no glasses, I could see it very clearly. It had purple, black and dark brown fur all over its body and was about nine feet tall. While I had initially thought the person was wearing a backpack I saw when it turned to face me that it had a large hump on its back and that it was just a part of its body. My mind was racing, trying to wrap my head around what I was looking at. I was there, in broad daylight, looking at what seemed to me to be a character out of one of the fairytales I read or the fairy-tale movies I watched on television all the time. There were small patches of white fur in areas too. The face looked exactly like a dog, like a pet dog that someone has in their house and that's when I realized it was some sort of dog because I had just seen it on all fours.

This must've been what the bear had been running from. The creature made a noise that sounded like a cross between someone sneezing and burping, it was the strangest thing. Its teeth were gigantic and looked seri-ously sharp. Its eyes were a normal blue color and it had claws instead of hands or even paws. I started to feel very dizzy and nauseous but there was nowhere for me to go. The creature made the weird noise one more time. It turned and then its ears perked up like it heard some-thing that I couldn't hear because I still wasn't hearing anything, aside from my own pounding heartbeat that is. Then it very quickly and almost before I even knew what was happening, got down on all fours and ran faster than anything I had ever seen move before. It went into the water and was across the large lake within no time and then it ran off on all fours into the woods. I started trembling so badly I almost fell into a heap right there where I was standing. I started hyperventilating and couldn't breathe. I was looking all around and up and down, and I think I was just completely and totally in shock. My young brain couldn't comprehend what I had just seen, and I felt like every muscle in my body was misfiring as it tried to make connections where there were none. There were none because what I just saw had been so unnatural and didn't belong here on this planet or in this world and I had come within mere feet of it. The thing scared a bear enough that it ran for its life. That should say everything right there. Suddenly I heard someone calling my name and it sounded like it was coming from very far away. I looked all around and finally focused on someone standing right in front of me. It was one of the mothers of one of the kids I played with from the upscale development. She shook me gently by the shoulders and asked me if I was okay. I muttered something unintelligible, and she told me no one was supposed to be out there because there had been reports of wild animals, mainly bears, running out of the woods and going right up to people trying to take their food. I nodded lamely and muttered incoherently again. She told me to follow her, and I did. We got to her car, and she drove me home. I don't know what she had been doing there and I never bothered to ask. She returned me to my mother who was obviously very concerned. I was able, eventually, to convince everyone that a bear had come right up to me, and they all assumed that was what had terrified me. I'm finally telling the truth now and that's only because I recently found one of those kids I used to play with from the development and it turns out several of them had seen the exact same creature in their yards or the surrounding woods over the course of a few years, back around the same time. None of us ever spoke of it when we were kids though. I guess that's not something you want to tell someone who you don't know too well when you're already wanting so badly for someone new to like you in the first place.

FOUR

SHADOW BEINGS

I WAS CAMPING out in the middle of nowhere in Indiana one summer when I had a terrifying experience with something that I still can't explain. It was 1996 and I was out there just to enjoy the warm weather in one of my favorite local camping spots in some woods near my home in rural Indiana. I tried to get out there as much as I possibly could because it relaxed and soothed me. It wasn't unusual for me to be out there, and it wasn't any sort of special occasion or anything like that either. The area where I was camping is one that I had gone to many times when I was growing up with either my parents or my friends as I got older. My boyfriend at the time and I had gone to this spot in the woods many times before too. I tried to make it a point to go out there and spend a couple of nights by myself from time to time as well and that's just what I was doing that night. I was there for three nights and four days. There was what we called a "swimming hole" in the area, in the woods, and I loved that the water was always cold, no matter how sweltering the heat was outside. It was like that one spot where the water just never seemed to be able to be warmed by the sun. It's unusual but not in a scary way, at least not before this happened to me, but it was more like it made the palace more quirky, special, and unique. I had hiked to the spot, leaving my car parked on some grass and hidden by some bushes near to the main road. The main road didn't have any sidewalks and there were no homes or businesses in any direction for about a mile. It was very isolated and very dense, and I felt like I was in heaven and had found true peace while I was out there. Well, that was all about to change for me and my ideas about the world were about to change as well because I had never been a believer in the paranormal. It really was just that I never gave it any thought, one way or another. It never occurred to me to fear something like a ghost or other entity, and I wasn't even sure I believed in the devil at that time in my life, and I wasn't by any means a religious person. My views on religion have changed drastically though and it was this experience I am about to share with you that made me a believer not only in things like ghosts and spirits but in God and the devil as well.

I had a good fire going, not one that was too big, but it was just enough for me to be able to make s'mores and read by its light. I was getting tired and when I looked at my watch it said that it was eleven o'clock at night. It had been an extremely hot day outside that day, and I had hoped that it would have cooled down by the time I went to bed. However, that didn't happen as much as I would have liked it to. It had gotten a bit cooler, sure, but it was still a little too hot for my liking, as far as my preferences for temperature when I went to sleep. Regardless of all that, I crawled into my tent and decided to call it a night. I figured if it got too hot out there, I could just walk the quarter of a mile to the swimming hole and cool off. It wasn't just the water there that was always very cold but the air around it too. It was cold in all directions as far as four of five feet away from the strange, shaped swimming hole. When people think of a swimming hole they usually think of some sort of circular or oval hole in the ground but this one had an odd shape that made it even more appealing to me. I was a person who never felt like I fit in with what society labeled as normal and so I looked for anything and everything that also seemed different and comforted myself with those people and those things, knowing I wasn't alone in my uniqueness. Anyway, I went right to sleep despite the heat but woke up at two in the morning freezing. I hadn't even thought to bring a blanket with me because of how high the temperatures were supposed to have been, and were up until that point, even in the middle of the night. I immediately crawled out of my tent but when I did, a couple of things happened that scared me.

The first thing was that I immediately felt like someone was intensely watching me. I couldn't put my finger on why I was feeling that way, but I just felt it and I knew somewhere deep down inside of me, maybe in my intuition, that someone else was out there. I tried to think about it rationally and would have easily been able to convince myself that it was possibly a predatory animal but the fact that it was also freezing cold all around my tent, for about a foot or two in all directions, made me start to think something really wasn't right. I didn't know exactly what was wrong but the extreme temperature change once I stepped out of that little one-to-two-foot barrier around my tent was very confusing. I stepped three feet away from the tent and I walked further into the woods to answer the call of nature as quickly as possible because of my fear but when I did, it was back to being unusually warm. I was confused, to say the least, but I decided to just climb into the sleeping bag I had previously been using as a cushion between the bumpy and rough bottom of my tent and my body, and zip it around me as a blanket to keep warm as I went back to sleep. I think it was all just so odd that I didn't even want to know what was going on. Unfortunately for me, something had other plans for me that night and I wouldn't be allowed to simply ignore what was happening all around me. I got nice and comfortable and tried turning off my brain but before I closed my eyes, I saw something that startled me. The moon was very bright that night as well as the stars and they provided a lot of illumination all around on the outside of my tent. I saw some sort of shadow go past my tent and from where I was lying it looked like it was in the shape of a person. I jumped up and looked out of my tent. I saw a white shadow running very quickly around the trees and then it stopped in front of my tent, just inches from where I was staring and peeking out of it, and it looked down at me.

My eyes went wide, and I didn't know what to do. I couldn't just back up into my tent and leave whatever that thing was standing there, especially because it had just seen me and therefore knew I was in there and because I was too afraid to move. It darted away and disappeared right before my eyes behind some trees further off into the woods. I knew it wasn't just hiding behind the tree as I literally saw it dematerialize, little by little, right before my eyes as I watched it. I got out of my tent because I no longer felt safe inside of it. I had no idea what was going on and curling up inside of a tent made me feel much more vulnerable. It was still freezing in that small circumference around my tent. I grabbed my sleeping bag and pulled it out of the tent. I then lit a small fire and tried to lay down and get comfortable again. I lit the fire at first just to have some more light for myself to be able to see, I had a flashlight right next to me within reach as well but suddenly it was freezing all around me and the fire was also providing me with warmth. I didn't sleep that whole night. Every time I would start to fall asleep, I would hear strange voices and whispers coming from the forest. I hadn't seen anyone else at all on my way to where I had set up my camp and for the most part the voices sounded like they were coming from very close to me and yet there was no one within my eyesight that could have accounted for them. Even if there were other campers or people who were otherwise in that forest in the middle of the night, wide awake and talking, with the proximity to where I was laying, I would have seen them somewhere. I looked all around and even got up with my flashlight to shine it all around in the woods but didn't see anyone there. The voices sounded like those on one of those old bulky-backed televisions when the station wasn't coming in properly and everything sounded and looked like static. I was terrified but knew there was nowhere I could go. I couldn't hike to my car in the middle of the night through the dark woods because, with what I was experiencing at that time aside, I also knew there were dangerous animals out there that would love to come upon a helpless human being that it could attack, eat, or otherwise hurt severely. I could have been killed and it wasn't a risk I was willing to take.

This is where the real terror started for me. After the second time I had gotten up and looked all around the woods with the flashlight for the source of the odd voices, I decided enough was enough and laid down with my eyes closed. I wasn't playing games with who or whatever was out there anymore and was angrier than anything that I was terrified in my most favorite place to relax and find peace and that I felt so helpless and victimized because of something I couldn't even see or otherwise prove was there. I yelled out some choice obscenities into the woods and made the mistake of challenging whatever was out there to show itself. That's when I started seeing shadow people. They weren't like the original shadow I had seen out there that night which had been white and quick moving. These ones were randomly appearing next to all the trees and all around the woods. They were literally just popping themselves into existence. They all had red eyes and with the appearance of each one, the static sounding whispering got louder and louder. I sat straight up while still inside of my sleeping bag and just sat there, trembling in fear, and yelling for them to leave me alone. I couldn't make out a word they were saying but I felt the evil coming off them without having to know what they were saying. I looked at my watch and saw that it had stopped at around two thirty in the morning, which is when I saw the first shadow being. I was utterly confused, and I started to feel sick. I threw up several times and it seemed like the more fearful I became the more shadow people appeared. I couldn't get up and go too far to vomit either because those evil beings were all over the place right beyond my camp. They were fully illuminated in the moonlight but even when I aimed my small flashlight at them, I could tell that they were solid individuals and not real "shadows" as we are taught our whole lives to think of them. I started to cry but that also seemed to make the activity even more prevalent and overwhelming. It dawned on me all at once that they were feeding off my extremely negative emotions. I don't know what planted that thought into my head, but I know it wasn't me who originally thought of it. It was the nineties, and I had no way of knowing about shadow people because nobody was talking about them back then. It wasn't at all like today when you could just look something up.

It empowered me to get angry once I realized what they were doing, and I forced myself to look away from them and at the ground. I sang songs I loved in my head and thought about the people and things that made me the happiest. I even smiled a time or two and within fifteen minutes of doing that, I looked up and just as I'd hoped, they were all gone. Not only that but the intense feeling of being watched, all the strange and extreme cold spots were gone and none of the entities were there. I knew they were completely gone, at least from those woods by where I was. My adrenaline must have come to a startling crash because I did fall asleep that night and I woke up at around seven in the morning to the sun shining brightly down on me. I didn't waste a moment and packed everything up to leave as quickly as possible. I don't go camping alone anymore and I never went back to that spot at night. I would go during the day but always with friends and always just to swim in the swimming hole. I've had issues with shadow beings ever since that experience though and they come and go from my life randomly and without any rhyme or reason. I've tried so hard to find some way to get rid of them, but I haven't come across anything that works yet and believe me I've tried everything. This whole experience has had a profound effect on my life, and I wouldn't wish any of it on my worst enemy. Thanks for letting me share.

FIVE

THE POLTERGEIST

BACK IN THE nineteen eighties I worked as a security officer at an old, shut down and abandoned summer camp. I oversaw patrolling the area where the cabins were. Though the camp was in the middle of the woods and far out of the way of any towns or other inhabitants, sometimes I would get a radio call that one of the care-takers or someone otherwise employed to do some sort of work on the cabins, or the land would hear something suspicious in the cabins. It was usually one cabin where all the suspicious activity was reported. Though it was several miles in either direction to the nearest town, one of those towns was a crime infested hellhole that was known nationally for its extremely violent crimes and terrible poverty rates. So, every time I would be radioed about something happening in any one of the cabins, I would immediately ride my all-terrain vehicle through the woods if I had to just to make sure everything was on the up and up and that no one had broken into the place. It wasn't unusual for me or someone else who worked security on other nights and at other times, even during the daytime, to hear strange noises coming out of the cabins as well, again with the one cabin being the center of most of the strange activity. There would be screaming and howling heard echoing through the woods or the sounds of banging like someone was throwing things and shattering glass. The list goes on and on of the reported activity in that one cabin. In fact, just that month alone we had one of the groundskeepers and one of the security guards run out in the middle of their shifts and never come back. They would never speak about why they had done such a thing except to say that they wouldn't ever go back there for any reason or under any circumstances. I always prided myself on being a rationally thinking man and thought the men were being rather silly in thinking that ghosts were real or that a place could be haunted by them or any other unseen beings. That was until I had my own brush with the paranormal that there was no way for me to explain away, rationalize or chalk up to an overworked and over-tired imagination.

I was working the overnight shift and the new

owners of the property were renovating everything. They were adding cabins and remodeling the ones that were already there, adding more recreational rooms and areas and things like that. They were hoping to have their grand opening the following summer which was only six months away. They were making great progress and most of the time there were crews there doing or fixing or building one thing or another, but I remember on that night, because it was a Sunday, it was just myself and one caretaker there on the entire property. There was electricity but the place hadn't been completely rewired so most of the cabins didn't have it yet. The caretaker's cabin and the one recreation area had electricity, the mess hall, and the bathrooms but that was about it. There were giant spotlights that were motion activated around each of the cabins and all the other buildings, but sometimes they didn't work either because like I said, the whole place needed new wiring. It had been a Catholic camp in the nineteen forties or fifties, something like that, and they were very frugal with spending on the camp back in those days, I guess. I was kind of dilly-dallying around, riding my ATV over some snow berms that night, when suddenly I heard the voice of the caretaker telling me that "Cabin twelve is at it again." He sounded so scared I couldn't help but chuckle to myself after telling him, in a very serious and professional tone of course, that I would be right there to check it out. I hung around for another fifteen minutes before making my way over to the somewhat infamous cabin. I didn't see the caretaker out there, but I decided to look around. There were no footprints in the snow anywhere near the place and all the doors and windows were completely locked. The lights were off and there were no sounds or anything like that coming from the cabin. He had reported to me that he heard screaming and banging, and that the lights were flickering on and off. I decided to go and find him to tell him what I found.

I went to his cabin, which was located a few doors down from cabin number twelve and I told him what I had noticed when I was there. It seemed like no one was there and that no one could have been there because they would've left behind footprints in the snow. He didn't believe me, and I could tell he was really scared. He didn't drink or do drugs as far as I knew but he looked so terrified that I started to become concerned that maybe he had taken something. I asked him plainly if he was under the influence of any mind-altering substances and he got very offended. He told me to go and check again, one more time, for his own peace of mind. I normally would have just told him I would go and check, but I felt bad for offending this very old and normally very kindly old man. So, I got back on my ATV, and I drove back over to cabin number twelve. I still saw no footprints in the snow aside from my own but as I circled around the cabin to the back, it was obvious that now the back door was open and the bathroom window, which was in the back of the place, had a light shining through it from the inside. My adrenaline immediately started to pump through my body, and I became almost excited because maybe he had been right all along, and someone was in there trying to steal the copper piping or squatting in there. There was someone in there, or so I thought based on the evidence of what I was seeing with my own eyes. I should mention here I also don't drink or do drugs and I didn't at that time in my life either. I was proud of my job and took it very seriously. I drew my taser and my flashlight, we weren't allowed to have firearms, and I walked up the three steps to the small front porch. I listened by the door for a minute and heard what sounded like whispering and giggling but I couldn't make out if it was a male or a female or several of either. It sounded like more than one person though and so I banged on the door and announced myself. I ordered whoever was in there to come out with their hands above their heads and in plain sight. I waited a minute or two but didn't hear anything and no one exited the cabin. I went around the back, thinking whoever it was must've gone out that way but there were no footprints there either. I could have easily chalked the back door being open to something being wrong with the lock. I could have convinced myself of anything, really, if I hadn't heard someone in there whispering and giggling. I went inside of the cabin.

I walked all around the downstairs and didn't see or hear anyone or anything. I took my time and tried to be as quiet and stealthy as possible. The cabins in that area were for the staff and were two stories and much larger than the cabins on the other side of a small clearing that was located beyond the connected backyards. I stopped at the bottom of the stairs and listened intently but at first, I didn't hear anything. Then, all at once I heard a woman screaming at the top of her lungs, as though someone were hurting her, and I also heard loud crashing and banging sounds. They sounded like they were coming from all over the upstairs and I couldn't pinpoint which room up there they were coming out of. There were only two small bedrooms and one small bathroom up there. I announced myself again and ordered whoever was up there to come out with their hands above their heads. The noises once again stopped, and I quietly and carefully made my way up the stairs. I was trying to wrap my head around how people could've gotten inside of the cabin without leaving behind any footprints or vehicle tracks. It occurred to me that it had only been snowing for a day and a half and perhaps whoever it was had entered the building before it started snowing earlier the previous day. I got to the top of the steps, and everything was still completely silent. You could have heard a pin drop in that place at that time. I walked to the bathroom, which was right in front of me at the top of the stairs. It only contained a toilet, a small shower that had no shower curtain or liner in it and a small counter. I didn't see anyone there. There was no closet. I moved on to the first bedroom on the right and saw that the door was closed. I banged on the door and once again announced myself and ordered whoever was in there to come out. I got no answer and decided to bend down and look through the peephole in the door's keyhole.

I didn't see anyone in there but knew I would have to open the door and check in the closet just to be sure. I opened the door slowly and immediately checked behind it. I checked the closet, and the room was all clear. There was no one there. That only left the other bedroom. I hurried over to it through the tiny hallway to make sure the perpetrators didn't try and escape quickly, before I could get there and while I was busy searching the room, I was already in. I slightly ran as I made my way to that room and noticed, once again, that the door was closed. I was reluctant to look through the peephole again so I just kicked the door as hard as I could so it would open and give no one a chance to escape. In hindsight I know all the things that are wrong about doing that but at that moment I was scared, and I didn't know what or who I was going to find there. Being in a completely dark cabin in the middle of nowhere in the middle of the night with nothing but a taser to protect you can really change your perspective on things. As soon as I kicked the door the screaming started up again and all the lights in the cabin started blinking on and off. The screaming was accompanied by loud and thunderous bangs that made the whole cabin shake. Every inch of me wanted to turn and run out of there as fast as I could and never look back, but I wasn't willing to give in so easily. I knew what everyone said about the other guy in my position who did just that and it wasn't good. It wasn't the reputation I wanted to have either. Also, I was still trying my best to think rationally about everything. I went over to the closet and looked in it but there was no one there. There wasn't much furniture in the rooms and no beds so there wasn't anywhere for anyone to hide. I turned to leave but something struck me in the back of the head.

I turned and saw hangers coming out of the closet and flying of their own volition and striking me all over my body. I ran out of the house as the screaming got even louder and started to sound more sinister. I got outside and looked all around the cabin as the activity was still going on and once again saw no footprints but my own. Suddenly and all at once, after I had walked around the entire cabin one more time, everything just stopped. I was standing there in front of the cabin but not on the porch. I was about twenty feet away from the steps that led to the porch, and I saw something move out of the top left window. That window was the one in the bedroom where I had just been attacked by some unseen force throwing hangers at me out of the closet. There was a figure standing there in the window and even though there were no lights on anymore in the room, the hallway light must've still been on because there was a soft glow illuminating her from behind where she stood in the window. She wore black and a black veil. She grinned devilishly down at me. I was so scared I thought I was about to have a heart attack. Then, suddenly, I heard a woman's scream. It was the same scream I had been hearing the whole time while investigating the activity and she immediately vanished. A tall shadow figure replaced her. It happened without any transition, so it was like she was there and then she wasn't, and the shadowy creep was. It had glowing red eyes and wore a fedora style cap. I got on my ATV and hightailed it over to the caretaker's house to tell him everything that had just happened to me. I kept working there but never investigated cabin twelve ever again. The caretaker that worked alone with me there on Sunday nights knew not to bother me with it because I wouldn't be investigating and there was so much activity in that cabin, I honestly don't know how they ever opened that camp, or that cabin, to the public in good conscience. It was horrifying. When I tell people this story, they insist that I should look up the land or if anyone had been murdered in or near that cabin or the woods. I tell them all the same thing and that's what I don't want to know. I really don't. I worked there for another year and a half before meeting the woman I would marry and moving on with my life. I became a police officer and let me tell you I am a firm believer in the paranormal now, not only since this encounter happened to me but especially since seeing some of the things I have while on my job as a police offi-cer. That's all for now. Thanks for letting me share my story.

SIX

SHADOW CREATURES

I HAD my very first encounter with something strange in the woods when I was only thirteen years old, but I've had many more ever since that day. I am convinced that whatever that thing was that I saw out there that night opened me up somehow, as in it opened my brain or my eyes, maybe both, so that I am more able to see things beyond what most other people can. I think it made me be able to see things beyond our own world, if you will. I was riding my quad through the woods near my house. I had been out riding quads with three of my friends pretty much all day that day and I was making my way home by taking a shortcut through the woods. There really weren't any other options for me besides leaving my quad at my friend's house and walking and that didn't make any sense because we all knew that cutting through the woods was the fastest and easiest way to make it from one point to another in our very small town. It was dark outside and late at night, but it never even occurred to me to be afraid of anything out there. I had grown up playing in those woods or otherwise being in them and had even gone camping in them with my family from time to time. The population of the town I lived in was very low and everyone knew everyone else and there were never any strangers. New people hardly ever even moved into the town, so we all knew one another, and all the adults looked out for all the kids, whether you got along with their parents or particularly liked the kid or not, if you were an adult in that town, you watched out for other's kids. I was familiar with all the wildlife out there and that didn't faze me either. When I left my friend's house that night it was just like any other night, and I was about to do something I had done a thousand times before. I didn't even give it a second thought and neither did my mother when I told her I was on my way home. It would've taken me a half hour to get from my friend's house to my house. She offered to come and pick me up, but it was more fun to ride the quad I had just gotten for my birthday than to ride around in my mom's embarrassing old and rickety station wagon.

I remember taking my time because I was filled with

adrenaline from hanging out and getting into little kid mischief all day long and I knew when I went home, I was expected to have a snack, shower, and then go right to bed. It was a weeknight and I had school the next morning. I knew every inch of the part of the woods that would take me from where I had been to where I was going that night but for whatever reason, maybe because of the above-mentioned extra adrenaline, I decided to take a different route. I figured that I would be okay because I was familiar with basically that whole area. It was a choice I would live to regret.

I was riding along and minding my own business when suddenly I heard a loud noise that sounded like it was coming from directly above me somewhere. It was clicking, sort of like the sound your car will make when the starter is bad and refuses to turn over for you. It had to have been deafeningly loud because my quad was very noisy, and I heard that clicking as though it were being done right in my ear. I stopped the quad and looked around. I didn't see anything out of the ordinary and I didn't hear anything either. Then, my vehicle started sputtering and shut off on its own. I knew I couldn't have run out of gas and was immediately nervous. I wasn't completely sure about where I was and now, I had broken down. I got off the quad as the head-lights went off and started checking it to see what the issue could be. I prayed with all my might that it was something simple and I could get it moving again right away. I was suddenly in a rush to get home. As I was crouched down and looking the quad over, I heard a loud thumping noise and felt a whoosh of air all around me at the same time. I got the chills, the hair on the back of my neck stood up and I immediately jumped up and looked around. There was literally nothing. That's when I noticed the forest had gone completely silent and there wasn't a single animal not only to be heard, but there wasn't one to be seen anywhere either. I couldn't shake the feeling of being watched and I'll admit, I was very scared at that point.

I wanted to get out of that spot so badly and felt so compelled to do just that, that I started pushing the quad from behind just so that I could move it somewhere else to check it. However, the woods never seemed to come back to life after that. I stopped for a minute to catch my breath and that's when something heavy fell out of one of the trees, from right above me. I felt that same gust of wind and heard the same loud and heavy thump that I had heard previously. I was terrified and didn't know what to do. I was already nervous and trying to focus on figuring out where I was so I could figure out where I should go to get home and I was silently screaming at myself for getting off the usual path and being a dumb ass. I didn't see anything at first and then I thought that something moved behind the tree where it felt and sounded like something had just fallen out of. There was a little bit of snow on the ground but not much and it didn't seem like, if something did fall out of the tree, it left any footprints or imprints of where it landed. I was scared but looked behind the tree anyway and once again, there was nothing there. I desperately needed to get out of there so I tried to see if the quad would turn over and start working for me, but it didn't. I was more than mildly frustrated as I pounded on the dash of it and yelled. I continued to push it but immediately heard footsteps coming up behind me. I whirled around as fast as I possibly could but again, there was nothing and no one there. I heard a strange noise that sounded like scratching on the tree right next to me and I moved away from it quickly. I felt as though I was losing my mind and really thought that I was going crazy or something. I stood there for a moment and once again heard a very loud thump and felt that strange breeze at the same time. That was the third time it had happened, and I stubbornly and somewhat stupidly decided I wasn't going anywhere until I figured out what the hell was going on. I would live to regret putting that out there like that.

I saw what had come out of the tree that time. It landed on its feet right in front of me. I had been looking to my left, towards the tree when it happened, and as soon as I turned my head, I was looking at what had not only caused the entire forest to go silent- or so it seemed- but also what had been stalking me the whole time I had been out there. I was standing at the back of my quad because like I said I had been pushing it along, and the figure dropped out of the tree right in front of it. It was seven feet tall, at least, and it was all black. It wasn't a shadow though, not how we normally think of them anyway, because I couldn't see through it. It had the regular shape of any human being for the most part. Its head looked relatively normal as did its arms and legs. There were no features or glowing eyes. It was simply all black. The hands were the most terrifying though as they were the least human hands I had ever seen or even imagined. They were literally claws and at that moment I realized it had climbed up the tree next to me before jumping out again right in front of me and that had been what the quick scratching sounds had been.

The reason I didn't say the head looked completely normal is because there was a set of strange horns coming out of it. They looked like the horns that belong on mountain goats, not on humans, and I remember thinking that they looked awfully sharp. I don't know what made me think to do what I did next, let alone what gave me the courage to, but I decided to ignore it. I pushed my quad past it as my heart was pounding almost out of my chest and I was silently praying with everything that I had in me that it didn't attack me. I moved around it and kept right on going. I heard the quick and rapid succession of it climbing up one of the trees next to me again and I had to stop because I was having a panic attack and couldn't continue pushing my quad and breathing at the same time. I thought for sure it was going to drop down in front of me again, with that very distinct and somewhat familiar thump and breeze, but it didn't. I got on the quad and tried it again, for what it was worth, and it turns out it was worth everything because it immediately started, and the headlights went on. I got out of there as fast as possible and eventually made it home. I hurried up and put the quad in the shed in my backyard before locking it behind me and turning to run into my house. As soon as I finished locking it all up, I heard that familiar thud and felt that familiar breeze. It had just landed on top of the shed. I ran as fast as I could into my house and locked the door behind me. I said hello to my mother and yelled goodnight to her as I ran up the stairs and into my bedroom. I locked that door behind me and looked outside to see if it was still there on the shed, but it wasn't.

I tried to go about my night as usual. I skipped the snack and just showered and went to bed. I was so scared I couldn't sleep, and I kept hearing that thudding noise on my roof. I swear there must have been at least five of them up there. There were all sorts of banging, but I just tried to ignore it and eventually I fell asleep. I woke up the next morning and my father was outside with his ladder. I asked him what he was doing, and he said he heard strange noises coming from the roof the night before. It hadn't even occurred to me that anyone else had heard the noises too, but I don't see why they wouldn't have. I think I just thought I was hallucinating or going crazy or something. I asked him if he found anything, and he said yes that he saw what looked like footprints of some kind. I asked him what he meant by that, my heart pounding in my chest as I waited for his answer, and he said it looked like someone or something wiped them away. He then mused that perhaps the wind had blown the snow around and that's what had distorted them. He didn't seem concerned at all that there were footprints on the roof. I asked him if I could see them, pretending I thought it was so cool and I was extremely interested. He allowed me to climb up the ladder to look while he held it in place and once, I looked I understood his nonchalance. The footprints had scrape marks going through them. I almost fell back-wards. They looked like the footprints of animals with claws or something like that, but I knew that the shadow demon things had merely been walking around up there on all fours.

That was the last I saw or heard of those creatures until I moved into my own house twelve years later. I haven't ever been able to get rid of them and still deal with them, among dozens of other entities I'll soon be writing about, to this day. I never found out what they are, and they've never done anything but land on my roof and make all sorts of noise. That's all I know for now, but I've been neck deep in research about shadow beings and creatures in the woods so hopefully there will be more information coming soon. That's it for now. Thanks for letting me share.

SEVEN

UNKNOWN HUMANOID

I WAS BORN and raised in North Dakota in the 70s and 80s, and it was such a different time to be alive back then. I remember one of my favorite things was when my family and I would all go camping in the woods. We wouldn't just camp out though, we would go on all kinds of scavenger hunts and have competitions. We went on so many adventures in the woods and would travel all over the state to see new things and search for new camps and areas where we could have even more fun. My parents had me young and they sort of grew up with me. One of the things they always loved to do and that we did often as well was night swimming. They couldn't afford for us to have our own pool in our backyard but a lot of the time when we would go camping, they would choose a place that had a lake or other swimming spot so that we could go on night hikes and then, we could night swim. When I had my encounter, I was hiking all alone in California, but I brought this up first so that you would understand my quirky habit of night hiking and being out and about, moving around the woods in the middle of the night. I would hang out at camp and sleep throughout most of the day and at night, at around ten o'clock, I would go and explore whatever area that I was in. I also tried to stay in places where there was a water source that I could swim in, but it didn't always happen that way, obviously. However, on the night I had my encounter there was a lake nearby. It was manmade and massive, and I swam in it during the day too, but it was a little crowded for my tastes. That's another thing I've always loved about the woods at nighttime and that's that you just don't see as many people. The lake was busy during the day but where I had set my camp up didn't have anyone else around it at all. I found a spot where there was no one else in any direction for at least a mile and I did that because I would have been leaving my stuff all by itself for the night while I was out wandering the woods. By the time this encounter happened it was the mid-nineties, and I was in my early twenties.

I traveled to California because I had a job interview for a new company I really wanted to work for, and my company gave me an all-expenses paid trip there so that I could represent them as well. It's a long and complicated story so I will spare you the details. I had some time to kill so decided to take a weekend and go into the wilderness and camp out. It was ten thirty and I had just extinguished my fire and got everything together that I would need to go exploring and for a nice and relaxing, peaceful, and quiet night swim. My parents, or at least my father, would normally have come with me but he had to work and couldn't get the time off. My mom wouldn't go anywhere without my dad. I never had any siblings and so I was used to being by myself anyway. I was single too at the time so that's how I found myself walking through a deep and somewhat dangerous forest in the darkness of the night, several states away from home when I had my encounter. I have seen some very strange and sometimes scary things in the woods throughout my life, but nothing ever compared to what I saw on that one night. My parents were big believers in the paranormal and they would always have friends over when I was younger to play with the Ouija board and I even remember attending séances from a very young age so of course I also grew up with a deep belief and big interest in those types of things. Cryptids never really were a thing back then, but I don't know if I ever would have cultivated such an interest in them had I not seen what I did that night. I was walking along a well-worn trail, but it was a different one than the one I had taken during the day to get to the lake. I passed a couple of other campsites that must have been set up after I did my mile walk around when I set up my own camp, but the people said hello and they all seemed friendly enough as we greeted one another, and I kept on going. I was about halfway to the lake by my calculations when I spotted in the beam of my flashlight what looked like a man peeking out from behind a tree. As soon as my flashlight hit the guy, his head popped right back behind the tree as if he were frightened of the light being shined right on him. I was nervous myself because the guy seemed extremely shady and suspicious to me because of the way he seemed to be hiding from me like that. It looked sort of like he had been planning on hiding and jumping out at someone but that I had caught him before he was able to carry out his plan. It just looked bad for him because whatever it was, he was doing, there's never anything good about hiding behind trees as people approach you in the woods. Especially when you're a grown man. I called out to him and asked him if he was okay. I tried to sound as friendly as possible, thinking maybe it was someone from one of the camps I had just passed who had maybe drunk a little too much or somehow gotten lost.

The man didn't answer so I lowered my light and tried again, but still, he didn't say anything back to me. I raised the light again because I couldn't see that far in front of me in the dark without the aid of the flashlight. I immediately noticed at that point that there was something wrong with his eyes. They were reflecting the light in such a way that it wasn't normal. I jumped a little bit as it startled me and when I lowered the light again and looked, I saw that the eyes still looked like they were glowing but that they were bright orange in color. I just stood there, not knowing what to do next as it finally started to dawn on me that I wasn't dealing with a human being or a man at all and maybe something paranormal or just out of the ordinary was happening to me. I didn't want to turn and run though I can't lie, my brain was screaming inside for me to do just that. I also couldn't just run forward on the trail and continue towards the lake because I would have had to have run right past the tree where this guy/thing was standing. It was still only peeking out from behind the tree but from where the eyes where it looked like it was about six feet tall. I am six foot and five inches tall, so I wasn't concerned about his size, though I did note that he/it wasn't small. I tried to be smart and think fast and I yelled out again, asking if he was alright. I will refer to it as a he until I get to what it was, just to keep things simple and easier to follow. I heard a response, but it wasn't what I had expected at all. The voice sounded almost like a hiss, and it said, "Come a little closer, your light is too bright for my eyes." I swear if the Harry Potter movies had been out at that time, I would have thought I had just come across Lord Voldemort in the woods of California. I was startled but I didn't lower the light right away and the hissing voice demanded, in that same tone, "Get that light out of my eyes and come closer so I can see you better." He was talking all the while still peeking out from behind the damn tree. I was starting to get really scared and I was also becoming confused. I understood where the fear was coming from, but I often wonder if the confusion was being put on me by whatever that thing was. I still don't know but if I had to guess I would say that it was messing with my mind.

I made the decision to take a few, very calculated steps towards the tree and to lower my flashlight. I aimed it at the ground, but I didn't turn it off. I took a few steps, making it so that the tree and whatever was behind it was only about five feet away from me instead of the original ten feet or so. It stepped out from behind the tree and that's when I realized I had made a terrible mistake. It turned out that it wasn't six feet tall at all and had merely been crouching the whole time we had been interacting. It was at least twelve feet tall. Its skin was all black and the eyes were a blazing color of bright orange. When it blinked, it blinked sideways, like a reptilian is said to and it simply looked down at me as I tried to understand the gravity of the situation, I had inadvertently found myself in. Its body in general, as well as the head and all its features looked perfectly normal as far as it had two regular legs and arms, a nose, a mouth, two ears- one on each side of its head and a nose in the middle of its face. It had a regular human-shaped head as well. But it was anything but human and I knew that right away. Like I said the skin was black and very tight around its bones, or whatever was underneath it. It wore no clothes and was very obviously a man. Its ears were a tiny bit pointed at the tops but not so much that it looked like an elf or something like that. It felt like an eternity that I just stood there like an idiot, staring up at it as it looked down on me with a strange glint in its eyes and grin on its face. Its hands were a whole other story altogether. There were five finger-like appendages, but they looked like thin knives with huge, pointed talons on the ends of them. Those fingers and the fingernails looked like they could rip me open in one swipe if it wanted to do that. I asked, "What are you?" It whispered back in that same voice, "A God" and that's when I ran. I ran as fast as I could with nothing but a flashlight illuminating my path. I made it to the lake and was far too terrified to go swimming or to turn back. I felt helpless and lost because there was no way I could just stay out there in the open for the entire night, but I also couldn't risk going back through the woods because who knew if there was more than one of that things or if it somehow had been able to follow me without my noticing it. I sat there on the ground and tried not to fall asleep. Eventually I fell asleep and had terrible nightmares about the creature in the woods I had just met. I woke up and the sun was shining, and there were tons of people at the lake again.

An old man came up to me and asked me if I was okay and I must have looked very startled because in response he randomly started explaining about all the tunnels that run under the lake and through the woods. He mentioned strange creatures and beings that have been sighted in those woods and at that lake for centuries and when he was done with his stories, he got up and returned to his spot in a chair he had set up near the water. I wanted to go and ask him some more questions about everything he had just told me, but I saw two little girls run up to him, both calling him grandpa, and so I just let it go. I hiked back to my camp, packed up my stuff and left the woods as quickly as possible. When I finally got home, I told my parents about what had happened to me out there and they both immediately wanted to start planning a trip to go out, just the three of us, with cameras and video recorders, to capture paranormal evidence of its existence or the existence of other creatures like the old man had mentioned. Believe it or not they did convince me to go but in the next few weeks, as we planned the trip and waited for the right time to head to California again, I started noticing terrifying shadow entity phenomenon in my own home which I had never experienced before. Shadow people weren't well known in the nineties and in fact no one ever talked about them. I thought I was going crazy. I canceled the trip and called a priest in to bless my home. I don't know what he did but it didn't work and ever since I have dealt with sporadic shadow being phenomenon everywhere I go. It comes and goes without warning and the more I learn about them the more I realize there's really nothing that I can do about any of it. I don't know how or even if shadow people are connected to what I saw that night back in the nineties, but I think it would be one hell of a coincidence if the two weren't connected, given when the activity first started.

PUBLISHER'S EXCERPT 1

I SAW BIGFOOT

SOUTH CAROLINA SIGHTING

So, I'm not really sure about the exact order of things that happened, but let me know if you think this is weird or not. I never realized what one of these things were until I started listening to your podcast a few years ago. I emailed you a while back, but I didn't share all of my experiences that happened at my childhood home where my mom still lives.

So, I grew up in Marion, SC. It's a tiny town about an hour away from Myrtle Beach. Population's around 6 thousand, and it's spread out. Mom's still out there in the country. Back then, we had two houses on our right, and one across the road from us, opposite a few fields. Country life, you know? To the left and behind our place, there were just fields for miles. Depending on the season, it'd be corn, soybeans, or tobacco. I got two older sisters, and we all lived in this small home with a barn-like thing we called the boat shed. Dad kept his boats, lawnmower, and stuff like that there. In our backyard, we had this big oak tree, and this massive magnolia tree in the front. Funny thing is, mom actually grew up on that land and moved back after she got married and had us.

We used to have these "prowler" issues, as my parents would say. Banging on windows, things going missing from the boat shed, and these "people" peeking into our windows. Now, let me tell you about one time. I was probably around 10 years old, and I had this major fear of the dark – whole different story why – and my big sis asked if I could spend a night in her room. My other sis and I shared bunk beds in another room, and we were super tight, like best buds. Me and the older sis, we had our moments, you know? She could be real mean, but sometimes she'd surprise me with some kindness. Should've been suspicious, really. So, I thought it was cool she was asking me to crash in her room, even though I was kinda scared of her.

Anyway, her room was like pitch black, only light was this red glow from her digital clock on the dresser. So, there we are, in our PJs, and she's telling me to get into bed. This bed's shoved in a corner, so you can only get in from one side. I crawl in, heart already racing 'cause I'm thinking, "What's she up to?" She's being weirdly nice, saying not to be scared, that she'll hold my hand till I fall asleep. I'm thinking she's planning something, like smothering me or something, LOL. So, we're lying there, it's a decently comfy bed, and she kills the light. I'm lying there, feeling better 'cause I can see a bit from the light coming through the blinds. She's like, "It's all good, I'm right here." I'm like, "Fine, whatever." I'm not sure why she's acting so chill, but it's late, and my eyes are getting used to the dark and the tiny bit of light.

I start drifting off, not sure how long I was out, but suddenly, I hear tapping. Even as I type this now, I'm feeling exactly how I felt that night, like 40 years later! I'm just looking around with my eyes, frozen with fear. I don't know why I'm so scared, 'cause I don't know what the sound is. I move my arm under the covers to feel if my sister's there, and yep, she's there, fast asleep. The tapping's coming from the window and it's getting louder and louder. I shift my eyes over, not moving my head, and I see this HUGE dark figure blocking most of the window. I'm holding my breath, feet freezing, realizing that's fear, right? I'm petrified. I think these "prowlers" are trying to break in. The blinds are kinda slanted down, so lying there, I can see a bit of whatever it is. All I can make out is that it's black and has these super white teeth. A big ol' mouthful of 'em, and I can hear it breathing, all raspy and gurgly.

I grab my sister's arm, whisper-shout, "Someone's at the window." She's like, "What?" I say, "Someone's trying to get in!" Trying not to move, talking real low. She shouts, "What?" I scream, "Someone's trying to get in!" She looks, sees the figure, and bolts out of the room, screaming for Dad. I slide out of bed, don't look back 'til I hit the floor, then crawl outta there faster than lightning. "Dad, Dad, someone's trying to get in the window! Hurry!" Now, Mom and Dad are asleep, but Dad jumps up when we scream, grabs his .38 revolver – yeah, he had that thing for dealing with these "prowlers" – and dashes out the front door in his underwear. Mom calls the neighbors, they grab their guns too and go help Dad.

Mom's convinced they're gonna accidentally shoot each other, but that's Dad. He comes back in a bit, saying he heard 'em running through the tobacco field, saw a dark figure breaking the stalks, but couldn't see details. And just like that, we're supposed to go back to bed like it's all normal. Yeah, right. I'm in the living room, sis goes back to bed, parents too.

I'm glued to the TV the whole dang night, totally freaked. I can still see it now, like I'm there. Can still hear it. Do I know what that thing was? Nope. But listening to your episodes where people talk about hooded folks or mysterious figures, it all comes rushing back. So, about a year ago, I went back to Mom's. Listened to some more of your guests' stories, talked to Mom – Dad's gone, passed away six years back – but Mom's still holding strong at 84, got my nephew with her, so she's not alone. She's got a load of stories from that house, which I'll share someday. Went back to that window where that "person" was ages ago, measured it up. No bricks or flower beds under there, just the hedges that were always there. The window's bottom is at 5 feet, and that thing took up the whole dang window!

So, I'm guessing it was like 7 and a half, maybe 8 feet tall, unless whoever it was had a ladder or something. Me and Mom just stood there, totally amazed. How did we just think that was a regular person? It hit me like a ton of bricks! Told a few close friends, got the "You're crazy" look and a grin, so I let it be. But I can't. The more I think about all the wild stuff that happened out there, something was going on, man.

————

I SAW BIGFOOT: BOOK 1

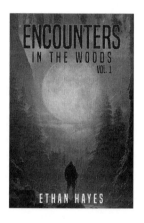

IT CAME AT NIGHT

It was the early summer of 1999, and after getting through a nasty divorce, I decided to move to get as far away from my past as possible. I didn't want to go to a city; instead I desired peace and quiet, somewhere in the countryside, away from people, lights, pollution, you name it. I just wanted some alone time to think through the past four years of my life.

I had always liked the mountains and knew there I'd find what I was looking for. I put most of my belongings in storage and set out to the mountains of Idaho to a small town called Stanley. I found a trailer to rent and settled in right away.

I hadn't moved into the trailer for a week before I was awoken by a loud slap on the outside. I shot up and looked around but couldn't see a thing, as it was pitch black. As anyone who's lived in the mountains can attest, when there's no moon, it's incredibly dark outside. Of course, this makes for spectacular stargazing, but seeing anything without the aid of a flashlight...impossible.

I sat there and listened for a repeat sound to make sure I wasn't just dreaming, but it never came. I nestled back into the covers and went back to sleep.

The next morning, I awoke to find my trash can had been dragged from the side of the trailer and down to the woods; garbage was everywhere. I then knew I hadn't dreamt the sound and chalked it up to a bear. I gathered up the garbage and put the trash can back. I placed a large rock on top and even bungee corded the lid down. I went about my day and thought nothing of it.

That night I again was awoken by a loud slap on

the side of the trailer. This time I knew I wasn't dreaming and intended to scare the bear away before it got into my trash again. I tossed the covers off me, grabbed a flashlight I had left on the nightstand, and rushed to the front door. I flipped on the outside light and threw the door open. I clicked on the old Maglite and scanned the front yard. I saw the trash can was how I'd left it. I continued to wave the beam of the light around but saw nothing. Thinking as if the bear could understand me, I cried out, "Don't come back, you hear?"

Satisfied that I had scared the bear away, I closed the door and locked it, turned off the light, and went back to bed. As I lay there staring into the darkness, I felt a sense of pride. I had been raised in the suburbs, but now I was fast becoming a mountain girl and had officially chased away my first bear. I closed my eyes and fell back to sleep.

I don't know what time it was, but I was again awoken by a slap. This time it was at the head of my bed on the outside wall. I opened my eyes but didn't sit up. All I could think was the bear was certainly as stubborn as my ex was, and I'd have to be just as determined to get rid of him as I had my former husband. I swung my legs out of bed, grabbed the flashlight, and clicked it on. When the light splashed across the room, I saw something large step away from the window, which was just over my bed.

Startled, I recoiled and turned the light directly on the window, but whatever had been there was now gone. I assumed the bear was now peering into my window like a sick voyeur. Determined that I'd have to really scare it away this time, I marched to the front door, flipped on the outside light, and threw open the door. The cool air wafted in as well as an odor I wasn't familiar with. The best way to describe it is to say it smelled like old musty or moldy clothes. I cast the beam of the flashlight across the yard and instantly caught sight of something racing into the woods, and from the half-a-second glance, it appeared to be on two legs. I kept the beam on the spot I'd last seen it, but it was gone. I first thought it odd that it was on two legs but remembered that bears sometimes walk on their hind legs.

Like earlier, I hollered, "Go away and leave me alone!" I looked at the trash can and saw that it was fine. Hoping that was enough, I closed the door, but instead of turning the light off, I kept it on and went back to bed.

The next morning I woke to find nothing out of sorts and went about my day until later that afternoon I was out clearing some debris from around the trailer when I discovered two large indentions in the ground just beneath my bedroom window. I examined them more closely, and to my astonishment, they appeared to be large footprints. I shook my head, as I couldn't believe what I was seeing. How could those be footprints and massive ones at that? I didn't take a picture, as I didn't have a digital camera at the time, and if I were to go off of memory, I'd say they were at least fifteen inches in length and had to be seven inches wide. I could make out toes and would guess the prints were two plus inches deep. I stepped back, dumbfounded, looked up, and saw that my window was about eight feet off the ground. I clearly recalled seeing something move in front of the window, so that had to mean that whoever was standing outside my bedroom window was eight feet or more tall. A tinge of fear creeped up on me. None of it made sense. I then began to think it was my ex harassing me. That he somehow found where I lived and was now here causing me trouble. My initial fear gave way to fury and anger. I marched inside the trailer, picked up the phone, and called his mobile phone. The second he answered, I'd give him a piece of my mind.

The phone rang a couple of times and went to voicemail. Filled with anger, I left a scathing message and hung up. I set the phone back in the cradle and exited the trailer, feeling better about myself. I wouldn't tolerate him harassing me like he had during our last year in marriage. There was no way I'd let him take away from the peace and solitude of my new life.

The afternoon gave way to evening. I grilled a nice steak, popped a beer, and relaxed on a chair, looking north towards the Sawtooth mountains. As the sun set behind the mountains, I found myself gripped by a feeling that someone was watching me. I don't know how to describe why I felt that way, but I could feel it. My sixth sense was telling me someone was in the woods near the tree line. Curious if it was my ex, I got up from my chair, beer in hand, and went down to the edge of the woods. I looked around but couldn't make out anything in the dark shadows of the hulking ponderosas and aspens. I called out my ex's name and finished by saying, "If you keep bothering me, I'll call the sheriff. Do you hear me?"

Of course, there wasn't a reply; in fact, there wasn't any sound at all coming from the woods. I tossed the rest of my beer back and threw the empty bottle. I heard it land, waited for a second to see if I could hear any movement at all, then turned around and went back to my chair. I opened my cooler, took out another beer, popped the top, and sat down to enjoy one last drink before I went inside. I could feel the fatigue of the long day laboring around the yard wearing on me, and before I knew it, I was fast asleep.

I woke suddenly, my body chilled. I was surrounded by the dark of night. I looked around, fearful, as I felt a presence in the darkness. I had no idea how long I'd been asleep, nor what time it was, but something wasn't right. I wanted to get up and move, but I felt frozen in fear. My head swiveled around as my eyes desperately tried to make something out, but I couldn't see a thing except for the brilliant stars above. I craned my head in the direction of the trailer, but the light I thought I had left on was out.

Then I heard it. The sound of footfalls coming towards me from the edge of the woods filled my body with terror. I found the courage to get to my feet and, without a concern for what could be in my way, took off at a sprint towards the trailer. I reached the side, felt my way to the door, opened it, and literally leapt inside. I slammed the door behind me and flipped on the light. I peered through a window in the living room, which over-looked the yard, but didn't see anything. I began to wonder if I was now just hallucinating all of it. Had my divorce been so bad that I now had some sort of PTSD? It took me a few minutes to get my composure and calm down.

Feeling at ease, I went to the sink to get a glass of water. I filled a glass, raised it to my lips to drink, but froze when I peered over the glass. There standing in the window, its black eyes staring at me, was something out of a nightmare. I let out a scream, dropped the glass, and ran back towards my bedroom, thinking this was my safe space. I closed the door and sat down on the floor next to the bed, my knees curled up to my chest, with my arms wrapped around them.

I could feel my heart beating heavily. I knew what I'd seen was not my ex, nor was it a person; it was something else, something sinister looking and big. Because like my bedroom window, the kitchen window over the sink was the same height.

I rocked back and forth, thinking about what I should do. I hadn't thought of bringing any sort of weapon with me. Heck, I had nothing to defend myself.

A loud slap came from the outside wall to my left.

I jumped with fear.

Another loud slap came, this time on the opposite side. That thing was moving around the trailer, and here I was inside with nothing to protect myself. Feeling helpless, I began to pray.

Tapping on the window above my bed startled me. I looked up but saw nothing but a shadow; it was there and looking down on me, I could feel it. Filled with terror, I jumped to my feet and raced out of my bedroom. I darted for the phone, pulled it from the cradle, and dialed 911. The second the phone connected, I begged for help.

The operator told me to calm down and said that a deputy would make it out to me as fast as they could. She, however, gave me the disclaimer that it would probably take about thirty minutes. So much for life in the mountains, I thought.

A sound from the front door hit my ears. I looked and saw the knob turning left, then right.

"Go away!" I screamed. "Leave me alone!"

The 911 operator was still connected and told me to go find a safe place to hide and to expect the deputy as soon as they could make it. She also recommended that if I had a weapon, to get it. I put the phone down, grabbed a knife, and picked up the receiver. The operator told me to go hide, which I did. I dropped the phone and ran back to my bedroom. I drew the blinds and hid in the corner next to the dresser, the knife firmly in my hand.

I still don't know how long it took the deputy to get there, but as I waited, the slapping and bangs kept going on and on, only to stop when I saw the headlights of the deputy's car wash over the trailer.

It took every ounce of control I had not to embrace the deputy and sob in his arms.

After a brief conversation, he investigated the property but couldn't find anything.

I told him emphatically that someone had been outside taunting me, and I gave him a detailed description of what I'd seen in the window.

I could tell he was doubtful of my description; to be honest, I was too. While I had heard of Bigfoot before, I never paid it any attention, nor did I believe they existed. But the more I thought about what I had seen, I came to the only conclusion that what was terrorizing me was just that, a Bigfoot.

He stayed for about forty-five minutes but had to leave. Without finding any evidence of someone currently there, he told me to lock up tight and, like the operator, recommended I go buy a gun.

I watched him leave and prayed that whatever was out there would leave me alone. My prayers were answered, as the rest of the evening was quiet.

The next day I went into town and purchased a shotgun. If this thing was going to come back, I'd at least have the means to protect myself.

The evening came without any issues, as did the night, until once more I was awoken by an incredibly loud thud. This was different than the slaps; it was like something had punched the side of the trailer. I jumped from bed, this time grabbing the shotgun, and went to the corner of the room and squatted down. I hadn't bothered to wear pajamas that night because I had a good feeling I'd have a visitor.

The loud bangs gave way to the entire trailer shuddering as if the thing was trying to tip it over.

I was beyond terrified and didn't know what to do. I went to the phone and, like the evening before, called 911. The operator once more dispatched a deputy.

As I waited, this time in the darkened living room, the shotgun in my white-knuckled grip, I decided I had to prove I wouldn't be pushed around. I mustered all the courage I had, marched over to the door, turned on the light, threw open the door, leveled the shotgun up towards the sky, and screamed, "If you don't leave me alone, I'll shoot you!" I pulled the trigger.

To my right, just beyond the light, I saw the creature race across the yard towards the woods.

Feeling victorious, I decided not to let up. I pumped the action of the shotgun and once more fired into the sky. "Get out of here!"

I could hear the creature crashing through the woods, the sounds of wood cracking, and heaving footfalls.

Once more I pumped the shotgun and let out a blast. Each time I felt my fear ease up. There wasn't any doubt now that the creature was fearful itself and didn't like the sound of a shotgun.

My fear was now replaced with anger, an anger born of this thing thinking it could torment me, that it could disrupt my new life. No, I wasn't going to have any of that.

The same deputy arrived, but this time he found me in a different state of mind. Against his recommendations, I joined him in searching the property. We found tracks, but he dismissed their being from a creature and said they probably were some teenagers causing havoc. I tried to argue with him, but there wasn't any use. We also found a couple of sizable dents in the siding, no doubt from it hitting the side.

When he left, I was still outside, my shotgun still in my grip. I looked towards the woods and, for good measure, fired once more into the woods. I wanted to make sure it knew I meant business.

I went to bed feeling not as vulnerable. I also ended up not having more trouble that night.

The next day, I went into town to find an electrician. I wanted lights installed all around the trailer with motion sensors. I'd cover every inch and then some; however, I was met with frustration, as I couldn't get the lights installed for a few days.

I arrived home in the middle of the afternoon to find

my trash cans not just turned over, but the can itself crushed. I knew what had done it and knew then I was probably in store for some trouble that night. I cleaned up the mess, loaded the shotgun, and prepared for what most likely would be a siege.

To my surprise, nothing happened. I thought I heard some noises like walking around, but no hitting the side of the trailer.

Morning came and with it no issues outside. The next couple of nights were similar.

The electrician came and installed the lights, giving me a sense of peace. I hadn't had any trouble, and I clearly thought my show of defiance must have warned it from coming up to the house.

Later that night I woke to the lights on the north end of the property turning on. I jumped from my bed and peered out the window to see the creature walking briskly back into the woods. I kept watching for what must have been minutes; then the lights to the south end of the property came on. I craned my head but didn't see anything. After a few more minutes, the lights installed to the west kicked on. I raced to another window and looked out only to see nothing. I assumed the creature was literally testing the perimeter. This thought gave me chills, as it proved it wasn't just an animal but had intellect.

The testing of the perimeter went on for about ten minutes before ceasing for the rest of the night.

I got up the next morning, now determined to find out more, and the best place was to contact the landlord. I reached him and detailed what had been happening. He denied any knowledge but did give me the ability to break the lease early without consequence. I did just that.

While I felt empowered with my shotgun and the lights, my anxiety was riding high. I hadn't come all this way to the mountains to live like this. I packed up and left the next day and never looked back.

I've never since had any experience like that and still live in Idaho. I frequent the woods and hike a lot in the Frank Church Wilderness. I've not shared this story before but thought that after all this time and with the acceptance of Bigfoot increasing, it was time to let people know this creature does exist and can be an inconvenience if you're looking for peace and quiet.

————

ENCOUNTERS IN THE WOODS: VOLUME 1

EIGHT

WINGED HUMANOID

MY ENCOUNTER HAPPENED in 2016 when I was on my way home from a youth group at my church. The group was held at night and went from seven to nine. It consisted of a bunch of my friends from high school, and we would all go even though none of us attended that church. Some of us didn't attend church at all but it was just something to do on a Thursday night. I lived in a very small town that had less than five hundred residents in the midwestern United States. When it isn't football season, there's literally nothing to do here. The only rule for the group was that we weren't allowed to have our cell phones on during the entire time we were there. I was a kid who followed rules and took direction so on most nights I didn't even bother to bring it with me because that way I wouldn't have been tempted to use it.

Most of the kids followed that rule anyway, just out of respect for the church and all that. That night there was something else going on at the high school and my two best friends and I all had younger siblings who were involved with the event there. I think it was a performance of some kind for the drama club. My mother was supposed to come and pick us all up afterwards but right at nine pm the youth group pastor came and told me that my mother called, and I would have to walk home. I was a junior but hadn't gotten my permit yet and while my friends had theirs, they didn't have vehicles. Plus, when you have a permit, you must be in the car with someone who has had their license for five years or more. I wasn't allowed to get into cars with other kids my age unless my parents knew them or gave me permission so that left only one option, which was walking. My friends didn't want to leave me there, but it was better than the alternative which was walking through the woods to get home. It was so much easier to go through the woods because my house was located more on the edge of town and there were a ton of hills, I would have had to go up to get to it. The woods were trails and like I said, much easier. So, while my friends didn't want to just leave me there to fend for myself, they did. None of them had the same rules about getting rides from other high school kids and they took off on me. I told them I would call them when

I got home. I wasn't angry or anything, but I also wasn't going to break the rules and disobey my parents. There's no way in the small town we lived in that it wouldn't have gotten back to my parents that I got into a car I wasn't supposed to.

The woods were behind the church, and I immediately set out to start walking. I had only ever had to walk home once before, and it was very uncommon. It was within only the first five minutes that I started to really regret not having my phone with me. It probably wouldn't have gotten service, but I could have at least listened to some music while I was out there with it. Anyway, I was walking through the woods and minding my own business, but I felt uncomfortable from the very second, I stepped foot into them. I felt like someone was watching me and I know this is something that so many people say happens to them when they're alone in the woods and something terrifying is about to happen, but I think that's just because it's true and our human intuition is on point. I tried to ignore it and just made sure that I listened better than I normally would have and paid closer attention to my surroundings. It wasn't that the forest was completely silent or anything, but it was a lot quieter than I expected it to be. My house was also surrounded with woods, and I went for walks through them all the time and I know it should have been much louder, and there should've been much more activity out there, especially at that time of the night. I didn't have a flashlight but because of the time of year there weren't any leaves on the trees and the bright moonlight illuminated the way for me so that I could see where I was going with little to no issues.

It was going to take me about twenty minutes to a half hour to get home, depending on my pace, and even though I was very freaked out for reasons I couldn't quite put my finger on, I was walking slower than normal because I was trying to hear if there was anyone behind me. I thought maybe some of the boys who had been at the youth group and who had heard the pastor tell me that I needed to walk home might have seen it as a great opportunity to follow me out there and scare me on video or something. I was being cautious but there was some other feeling that was underlying the whole time as well which was the feeling that something terrible was about to happen and I couldn't shake it. Suddenly all the hairs on the back of my neck stood up and I stopped dead in my tracks. I heard a loud hissing sound. Even though the sound was exactly the sound a snake would have made, it was so loud and invasive that I knew the snake would have had to have been gigantic to have been so loud. The ground underneath me even vibrated a little bit because of the sound. I knew most of the animals and other wildlife in the woods in my area and I knew there were no gigantic snakes anywhere. The dread I had been feeling all along had been validated with that one sound, but I didn't know what to do. It sounded like it was coming from all around me, so I stayed standing where I was and looked all around. The forest was dark, but I could see a few feet around me on all sides. I spun around and looked in every direction, but I didn't see anything. I started slowly walking forwards again, towards my house. I picked up the pace a little but because I figured I already knew now that there was something out there with me and I just had such a horrible feeling about whatever it was that I no longer needed confirmation something was greatly amiss and just wanted to get the hell out of there.

I saw something moving up ahead of me and I once again stopped. I ducked behind a tree and peered around it, trying to stay hidden from view from whatever the thing was. It was squatting and hunched over but I only saw it as if it were a shadow because it was too far away. I must have gasped or something because whatever it had been doing it stopped and looked all around. Then, as I watched from behind the tree, it stood up and turned to face me. It was a hideous beast and like nothing I had ever seen before in my life. It was approximately ten feet tall and standing on two legs. It had regular arms that were muscular, as the legs were, and that weren't too short or too long. Its eyes glowed red and I could see that it had red all over its mouth. It sniffed the air which made me cringe and I wondered if it would smell me and then find me behind the tree and do God knows what with me. I was working myself into a frenzy and I could hear nothing at that point but my own heartbeat. It seemed so loud, and it was like, as soon as I had that thought about my heartbeat being so very loud, the being stopped, turned in my direction and looked right at me. It hissed at me and then gave me a sick and twisted smile of all black and very sharp teeth. I ducked back behind the tree, but I heard it grunting and I heard the leaves on the ground rustling. I thought for sure that it was coming right at me and that it was going to kill me or eat me or something. Its skin was dark gray and a little wrinkled and it didn't have any fur or hair. It had ears that reminded me of bats and a small and pointed nose. It had the head shape of a regular human being. Suddenly the movement that I thought was coming towards me stopped and after a minute more of listening intently I peeked back around the tree. I saw the entity, it was closer to me but not too close, and it looked at me again. It looked from me to the sky and back again several times and then it let out an extremely loud and ear-piercing squawking noise. It was so loud I thought that my ears were going to explode from it.

I could do nothing but stand there and stare at it, despite how desperately I wanted to run and hide or at the very least cover my ears. It looked at me and hissed one more time before gigantic black wings popped up from behind it. The wings were huge and were at least twelve feet off the ground even though they originated from the middle of the creature's back. They looked damaged and ripped up, with large and small holes throughout them. It looked up into the sky again and simply took off into the air as I stood there, stunned, and watching it. I watched it as it flapped its wings and flew off into the night and the direction it was going was towards my house, or at least that's what I thought. I couldn't be sure because I wasn't the best with directions. Also, I heard it squawk one more time. I didn't know what to do because I would have had to run in the same direction and all I could think was that it was simply waiting for the right time to swoop down and pluck me off the ground, carrying me off into the night with it. I ran anyway though, and I felt as though I were running for my life. I ran until I was completely out of breath and had no choice but to start walking again. I was about ten minutes from my house still and once again I just kept listening, as I walked very slowly, for some sort of noise or other indication that the creature had been following me or that it was still around. Hell, for all I knew there were more than one of them and another one had managed to find me. The only thing I heard was the silence of the forest. It was unnaturally quiet still, the hairs on the back of my neck were still standing and I knew because of those things that something was still out there with me. It scared me but I had no choice than to keep on walking so that I could get home. I knew I was being watched and had a fairly good idea of what was watching me. I knew then that the creature had merely followed me without me really noticing it. I finally made it home, but I didn't look up or into the trees the whole rest of the way. I went inside of my house, tried to say hello to my family as calmly as I could and took a shower. I went to bed without mentioning what had happened to me to anyone. I hadn't even called my friends. I wasn't sure if I wanted to tell them about it either.

I ended up not ever telling anyone until very recently. I came across some news online that reported sightings of a terrifying bat-like humanoid creature in my town, in those same woods. I still live here, in the same house with my parents and I haven't seen it since. I haven't really been in the woods since then either, but I've felt many times that I was being watched when I was otherwise out on a walk at night with my dogs. I think maybe it picked up my scent when it was sniffing the air the way it had been and that it can find me not if it wants to because of that. I told my two best friends so far and now I am writing it here. Maybe I'll tell my parents, but I'm worried they'll insist it was a demon or something. Who knows? I mean, maybe it was a demon or a devil, but it seemed somewhat human, almost and I just don't know what to make of it and live in terror all the time now since finding that information online. I know from reading other encounter stories that I'm by no means the only person who has ever witnessed such a creature, a winged humanoid, but what they look like seems to vary greatly across the board. I will write again if I have another encounter with it or anything else, but I am hoping and praying with all my might that it doesn't happen. I don't know if I could take seeing the creature again. It's truly terrifying.

NINE

DEMONS

WHEN I WAS fifteen years old in the 80s, I made money however I could on the side because aside from working for almost nothing at my parent's restaurant, I wasn't allowed to get an actual job. I would babysit and walk people's dogs and had gotten a reputation in my little neighborhood as a very responsible young woman who was in high demand for those types of jobs. The woman whose son I was tutoring asked my mother if I could house and dog sit for her and her family while they went away on vacation for a week. My mother talked to me about it, and I was so excited to be able to go and do it. She offered me what I considered a ton of money at the time, and I would get to be in a house all by myself for an entire week. I was a good student and on the honor roll so there was no worry about me inviting people over or having a party. I was a good kid, and these people were willing to trust me in their home and with their pets for an entire week and that made me feel good. Of course, I would have to check in over the phone multiple times a day with my parents and there was a whole list of other duties I was to see to while they were gone. I couldn't wait. I hadn't ever been to their house before because when I would tutor their son it was through a church program. They attended the same church as my family and so they would meet us there and the mother would do her volunteer work or otherwise run her errands while her son and I spent anywhere from sixty to ninety minutes together under the watchful eyes of other church volunteers. I knew they lived out on the edge of town, so to speak, because the address was one, I was very unfamiliar with but when she mentioned the lake I knew right where it was, and I knew the lake was out in the middle of nowhere. It was a little recreational area for people to go and swim and have fun during the summer months. I hadn't had much experience with dogs except walking them for my neighbors and my parent's friends, but I didn't think I would have many problems with caring for them either. I knew I was capable and so did everyone else, so I wasn't worried at all day I got into my dad's car, and he drove me out into the middle of nowhere to find these people's house.

It took almost forty-five minutes for us to find it and I saw that my dad was worried a little bit once we finally pulled up to it. It was massive and surrounded by woods. There wasn't a neighbor or another house for miles and the woods looked really foreboding in the darkness of the night. I got the chills, but my dad quickly reassured me, which I think was more of a reassurance to himself than anything else, and he walked me in. I found a list of emergency numbers and things I needed to do while I was there. The dog's feeding schedules were there and things like that and it said which room I should stay in while I was there. The house was old and drafty, but I fell in love with it right away because I could tell it was built a long time ago and loved history. My dad stayed for a few minutes and then he left, and I got to work feeding the dogs and putting my things away in the bedroom upstairs and at the back of the house. I had a clear view of the backyard and surrounding woods from the windows in the room and in one of them there was a bench seat that I could lay on and stare out at the sky or read a book. It was my dream come true at the time. Eventually it was time to take the dogs for a walk and I remember that I dreaded that task because normally I would just walk them along the street but there were no sidewalks and I couldn't allow them to just roam the yard until they did their business either because the woman was very clear and reiterated to me several times that she didn't want them doing their business out there. She said there was a clear trail that led from the back-yard and into the woods a little bit that once you got to a certain point it became a circle and when you followed it, it spit you out right back in the yard again. Like I said before the woods seemed ominous to me, but I was taking the responsibilities given to me very seriously and wasn't going to disobey the owners of the home and pets.

I put each dog's leash on it, there were two of them and they were some medium sized breeds. They were excited, of course, but when we reached the beginning of the trail in the woods they suddenly stopped jumping, running, and excitedly barking and started whining and backing away. It took pulling them forward to get them into the woods at all. They were very quiet and jumping at every little noise. I kept thinking something was moving out of the corner of my eye but when I would look at it straight on there would inevitably be nothing there. The dogs were sniffing around, and I was hoping they did what they needed to do quickly so that I didn't have to walk the whole trail and could just turn around and go back exactly the way I had gone into the woods. The dogs were taking their sweet time though and they both seemed nervous the whole time. I also felt like I was being watched the whole time and it was creeping me out, but I noticed a lot of owls in the trees and other little animals scurrying around, so I figured I was being watched but by the animals of the forest and not anything nefarious. Eventually I came to the circle in the path, but the dogs hadn't gone to the bathroom yet and there was a little bench there that looked completely out of place but that I just assumed the owners of the house had put there for occasions just like this. I sat down, never letting go of the dog's leashes, and watched anxiously as they continued to sniff all around and whimper at what looked like nothing at all. Suddenly the dogs both started barking and growling at some trees behind me but when I turned around of course I didn't see anything. Their fur and haunches were raised, and they were seriously freaked out and felt threatened by something out there that I couldn't yet see. I jumped up off the bench seat and turned around and that's when the tall man stepped out from inside of the thick trees.

He was unnaturally tall, standing at around ten feet and he was so thin it was more like he was emaciated than merely skinny. He wore a three-piece suit and a hat, with a cane held in his right hand. He stood there for a moment and smiled but when he did the dogs yelped and whimpered. They both gave up their aggressive stances and positions and fell in like right behind me. It was like they needed to be protected from this guy and I realized then they had either smelled or sensed that he was out there all along and that's probably why they had been acting so strangely. They were peeking out from behind my legs and one of them urinated right there next to where we were standing. It was disgusting but I didn't want to take my eyes off the smiling man. The look on his face was creepy but aside from the way he was dressed and how tall and thin he was, there didn't look to be anything out of the ordinary about him. Not at first anyway. I said hello and he responded in kind. His voice oozed fake sweetness and I was more frightened after he spoke than when he had first just randomly appeared. He took a couple of steps closer and asked me what I was doing out there so late at night. I told him I was walking my dogs and he looked at them with a look of disgust on his face and just nodded back at me. The whole time he didn't stop grinning that sweet but sinister grin. I immediately told him that I had to go but didn't want to turn my back on him. He was suddenly right in front of me, and I have no idea how he was able to move so quickly. I had barely blinked before he closed the distance of about ten feet. I was shocked and tried to turn and run but he had me by my wrist. His eyes were suddenly all black. His teeth were sharp and black too and he smelled like death. I started to cry, and he breathed in deeply as if the scent of my fear was almost too intoxicating for him to bear. Then his hand was on my throat before I even knew what was happening.

One of the dogs came from behind me and bit down hard and fiercely on the man's shin and he grabbed it and screamed out in pain. It wasn't a normal sounding scream though and instead it sounded like a distorted tape that had been played one too many times or something. It sounded evil and demonic, but I didn't stick around to see what happened next. I was running for my life and the dogs weren't too far behind me. The man could have caught up with us if he wanted to, but he wasn't behind us and all that was left of him was an evil-sounding laugh that permeated the air and seemed to be bouncing off all the trees in the forest at the same time. The owls and night critters had gone quiet. I didn't stop and ran until I reached the house. I got to the back door and before I went in, I turned around and saw the old man standing there, between two of the trees on the property line that separated the yard from the forest that surrounded it. I called my dad first and he called the police. Before long the cops and my parents were at the house but even after a thorough search, they couldn't find the man or any sign that he had ever been there in the first place. I kept thinking I was seeing him all over the outside of the house as they questioned me. I would see him standing behind a tree at some point and then I would blink, and he would be gone only to reappear a block away and standing right out in the open on the corner but despite my pleas for the adults to just look, they never saw anything. The police were very angry when they left because they thought I was just trying to prank my parents. My mother didn't want to bother the homeowners while they were on vacation, so she stayed with me for the rest of the week. This wasn't the last of my being tormented by the old man in the suit and in fact it was only the beginning. For years I had to deal with him visiting me everywhere I went and sometimes he would even appear in my room after a particularly evil and disturbing dream about him. I'll write more about the rest of the encounters at another time. I think he was either the actual devil or an agent of his, I can't be sure obviously. He was fully evil and demonic and delighted in terrorizing and terrifying me ever since that night in the woods.

TEN

SWAMP THING

IT TOOK me a long time to come to terms with what happened to me and that's not because I had a hard time believing it, personally, because I was there, and I know what I saw. However, no one else ever believed me and most people I talked about it in the beginning made me feel like I was insane or needed some sort of mental help. It wasn't cool to have encounters like this back in the nineties, and it wasn't until the internet became somewhat what it is today that I finally became comfortable sharing my story again. I grew up hanging out in the woods near my house and all over my town, just like any other kid in rural Louisiana at that time. I was a little bit different though from my peers and neighbors in that I had always had paranormal experiences. Granted my parents and the other adults in my life chalked them up to nothing more than my overactive imagination but it was just something I sort of learned to deal with and keep to myself. I would often camp out in the woods at night and my parents never had a problem with it and most often they didn't even know where I was. Because of how I was raised and the things I had seen for as long as I can remember, I was an outcast. Not only that but I became a lot more spiritually aware then most kids my age. I was twelve at the time and this encounter is what eventually turned me into a religious man later in life. I just cannot put a name on what it was that I saw except to say that it was pure evil and ancient.

There were a lot of urban legends in the town I grew up in and most of us kids did what we could to debunk them. In fact, I was only five years old when I had my first experience with what I believe was a demonic entity and it was while taking a dare for five dollars to spend two hours in the middle of the night and in the dark, in an old, abandoned house in the middle of the woods. My friends had parents like I had, for the most part, and so we were basically free to roam around all hours of the night and had no one looking after us. One night, after a particularly bad fight with my father, I stormed out of the house and was determined to get revenge by staying out in the woods all night long. I was too afraid to go back to the haunted house where I saw the demonic entity, but I knew the woods near it and surrounding the property were dense and dark enough that no one would be able to find me there. I ran out of the house, crying, and made my way over to the woods. There were woods everywhere in the town, but they were sporadically placed and only connected to homes periodically, all except for this one abandoned house. I got there and didn't have anything to sleep in or on or to keep myself warm or light my way. I considered going into the house, but it was warm enough outside and I figured if I really had to, like if anyone came looking for me, I could always change my mind and make my way inside of it. I found an old piece of cardboard in a dumpster in the backyard of the abandoned home, and I carried it into the woods with me. I was going to use it as a makeshift bed that night. I set it up but couldn't sleep. I thought the movement in the forest and the noises all the animals in the woods and the nearby swamp were making would keep me awake but it turns out there was nothing but silence that night. That was highly unusual and scared me almost enough for me to reconsider my terrible choice and go home for the night. Almost.

It struck me as so odd that everything was so still and quiet and made me so incredibly uncomfortable that I decided to walk around. I wanted to not only clear my mind and blow off some steam, but I also wanted to tire myself out. I walked and walked until eventually I came to the swamp. I didn't go right up to it but the sounds of the frogs and other animals in there were helping me to relax and I decided to curl up under a tree and lay down right there for the night. I hadn't brought the cardboard on the walk with me but didn't think it mattered as by that point it was already one in the morning and I was emotional and exhausted. The walk had worked along with the argument and other events of the day, to help me find a way to get to sleep. I was out before I could even give it a second thought. I woke up with a start to a loud and scary sound coming from the swamp. I couldn't tell if it was coming from around the swamp or inside of it but either way it was terrifying. It sounded like a giant, gurgling frog was somewhere there. I tried to shake it off as a regular and totally normal animal or amphibian and got up to use the bathroom. To do that, I turned my back on the swamp altogether. As soon as I was done doing what I had to do, I heard a loud splashing sound and then loud gurgling coming from a few feet behind me, right where the swamp was. I was already thinking that it was another ghost or other paranormal entity, and I wasn't looking forward to turning around to face it. I learned with goats and other paranormal entities that if you just ignored them and turned your back on them once you saw them, they would leave you alone and more than likely they would disappear altogether. That was my plan, but it didn't work out that way for me. I turned to face the horror I somehow knew was standing behind me.

It almost looked like a man at first. I didn't have a flashlight with me, but the moon and stars gave me enough light that I could make out the shape of it and most of the rest of it. It was around eight feet tall and muscular. It wore what looked like a man's wrestling suit with the shorts and the tank top/muscle strap things at the shoulders. It had a bare belly and chest and nothing on its arms or legs below the shorts. It looked like the material of your average wetsuit. The "man" stood awkwardly on two legs and his skin looked greenish and scaly. I noticed the tip of its tail waving back and forth behind it. I wouldn't say that the tail was wagging though because it was moving slowly back and forth. The tail was bright green like the scales on the rest of the man's body. I keep referring to it as a man because it also had a beard, which was green, of all colors and bushy green eyebrows. It had no eyelashes as far as I could see and its gigantic eyes that were much too large for its face were also bright green but with a vertical slit in them.

The color of the slit in the eyes was reddish orange and not black like I for whatever reason had expected it to be. It gurgled loudly and moaned pitifully as black slime and sludge came pouring out of its mouth. It just stared at me the whole time, unblinking. The creature then turned and jumped into the swamp with a loud splash. I ran as fast as I could back to my house and that was the end of that. I tried telling my parents, my friends and even my siblings but no one believed me, so I was determined to probe them all wrong. After I was done being grounded for running away, I went back out there. I am leaving out details here that aren't pertinent to the story, just so you know. I decided that I was going to take pictures of the creature and I had my tent and flashlight with me and was more prepared that second time. I got into my tent but I aimed my flashlight at the swamp and set it up so it shouldn't have fallen. I had a brand-new roll of film in my camera, which was within arm's reach. I didn't mean to fall asleep, but I did eventually.

I woke up to the sound of my dad angrily shouting my name. I knew that wasn't possible or at least that it wasn't probable because a month had passed by, we hadn't had a fight and he was the one who gave me permission to go and camp in the woods. I got out of my tent anyway though and called back out to him. He told me to get my butt over to him immediately and that I was in big trouble. It was his voice alright and so I hustled my butt off to try and make it to him as fast as I possibly could. The whole time I was too distracted by what I could have possibly done wrong to think of the creature/man or much of anything else. I left behind the camera. Eventually it came time for me to walk past the swamp. I immediately saw all different colored small orbs of light and stopped in awe to watch them. They danced right before my eyes for about five minutes before blinking back out again one by one. The sound of my father calling me and sounding angrier than ever snapped me out of it. It sounded close but I couldn't tell which direction it was coming from. I turned to walk away but before I could yell out and ask him where he was, something grabbed my ankle and started pulling me towards the swamp. I was terrified and screamed bloody murder for my father and for general help. I turned and looked at what was dragging me as I tried and struggled to get away from it and get it to release me and I saw a green and scaly human hand wrapped around my ankle. It was strong, whatever it was but I managed to use my flashlight, which was heavy, to smash into it until finally it let me go. I got up and ran to a nearby tree, but I couldn't move too quickly because of how sore my ankle was. I looked back and saw the green man/creature coming out of the swamp. It slithered out on its stomach and when it looked at me and flicked its tongue out it was forked, like a snake or other reptiles would be.

Its arms were down at its sides while it slithered my way, but it opened its mouth and looked like it was grinning as I heard my father's voice yelling for me, coming out of the creature. I was so confused, and the terror was unlike anything I had ever felt or experienced before in my life. Suddenly and all in one quick movement it stood up. It stood there, just staring at me, and emanating a very aggressive energy. I tried to run home as fast as I could, but my ankle seemed to have been sprained or something. I made it out though, but I had left all my stuff behind and got grounded again and was forbidden from going into the woods anymore for a long time. I didn't argue with my parents on that one and in fact I decided right then and there I never wanted to go into those woods, or anywhere near that swamp and whatever else was lurking out there, ever again. My ankle was just severely bruised both on the inside and outside of it, so I guess I got lucky in that it didn't manage to drag me down into the swamp with it to do only God knows what with me and that my ankle wasn't permanently damaged. I didn't even bother to tell my parents or anyone else what happened to me because of what had happened the first time when I tried to tell everyone, which is what got me into trouble in the first place the second time. That's all for this encounter but I will be writing about the demonic entity in the haunted house as well. Thanks for letting me share and finally get this out there.

ELEVEN
SHADOW ENTITIES

MY ENCOUNTER HAPPENED while I was snowed in in a cabin in Montana with my best friend from middle school and his family. Our parents were friends as well which was much more usual in the nineteen sixties than it is today, and it was no big deal for the two of us to go on vacations with the other's family. Occasionally, even our families all got together for vacations as well. One of my favorite things to do was go to the cabin with my buddy Billy and his family because unlike me, he was an only child. He had all the best of everything, and his parents were somewhat wealthy, at least when compared to mine. We planned on driving to the cabin which was several states away from where we lived at the time, both of us in the same town. Then we would stay at the cabin for a week and drive back home with the whole thing taking two weeks so that we could stop on the way there and on the way back to sightsee a little bit. However, it didn't work out that way because on the third day there a snowstorm rolled through the area, and we were all but stranded inside of the cabin. There was a huge yard and the woods that surrounded it and as ten-year-old boys that's really all we needed, and his parents didn't seem to mind so we just stayed and decided we would ride it out. It had been snowing in a blizzard for two whole days and when we finally got to stir crazy to be in the cabin anymore, his parents let us go out with the rule that we didn't traverse too far into the woods just in case it started storming again and we got lost out there. Now, we had been there a dozen times or more and were both confident that there was no way we could get lost out there, but we just nodded and agreed with what his parents said and bundled up to go on an outdoor adventure.

The woods looked very different covered in snow. It was early in November and a bit early in the season for such a terrific and brutal snowstorm, but we were just happy to be out there finally doing something. We had been there in the snow before but never when it had fallen to where it was almost up to our knees, especially in the backyard and the woods, where no one had been since the storm started and where no one had shoveled. We both set our watches to the same time his parent's kitchen clock said on it and promised to be home before dinner at six. It got dark right around that time too so that was one promise we fully intended on keeping. However, it didn't work out that way for us that night. We trudged through the yard to get to the woods and played several fantasy games about knights and cowboys of all things and before we knew it, it was time for us to start heading back to the cabin. We went much further in the woods than we were told, but Billy was adamant he knew the way back. I followed him but after walking in definite circles for about fifteen minutes, I started to get scared. He was my best friend and already knew that I was afraid of the dark. He never gave me a hard time about it because he and I were more like brothers than anything else, but I could tell he was annoyed that I was starting to whine that he didn't know the way back to the cabin like he insisted he did. We knew we had been to the spot we stopped at eventually a few times before because ours were the only footprints in the snow at the time. He and I stopped to think about things for a few minutes and decided to just go the other way, a way we hadn't tried yet, and hope it got us back on the right path to the house. We walked for another five minutes and that's when we started seeing the strange footprints and what looked like drag marks behind them all over the woods.

It couldn't have been a person because the foot was extremely thin but wide enough that we could see that it at least looked like the bottom of a foot and several toes. Those tracks turned into what looked like hooves, but both sets of prints had those same drag marks behind them. We were scared and confused but we were also hopeful. The way we figured it there was someone else out there and it was a human being, perhaps with some animal or something and if nothing else maybe they could point us in the right direction. On the other hand of that, it was private property, and no one was supposed to be there at all and that worried us because whoever it was obviously didn't care about trespassing. The sun had fully set, and it was very dark outside. Luckily the light from the full moon and a sky full of stars reflected off the snow enough that it made it a lot easier for us to see without flashlights than we would have otherwise been able to have it been a regular day and hadn't snowed the way it did. I was terrified but it got worse when we looked up and saw at least half a dozen sets of red eyes glowing and peering out at us from inside the trees all around us. I asked Billy what the hell we were looking at, but I think that was the point when he finally understood what my fear of the dark was all about and was just as scared as I was. He said he didn't know, and we wanted to run out of there but had no idea where to go. We felt like we had tried the only two logical directions and had nowhere to run without knowing the way. We started to hear growling and that's when I think we both just decided it was worth the risk to randomly run in a direction to better be able to get out of there and away from whatever was in the trees.

As we ran, Billy kept looking back to make sure that I was right behind him, and I didn't look back at all. He ran right into something hard and the way he fell backwards at first, with such force, I thought it had been a tree. I wish I had been right about that, but it turns out I wasn't. Standing in front of the both of us, what Billy had accidentally run into, was a gigantic, cloaked shadow being. We both stared at it as I tried to help Billy up off the ground despite my trembling and my terror. It was at least eleven feet tall, and its cloak dragged along the snowy ground behind it. Its eyes were bright red and glowing but there was nothing but drag marks behind or around it. It hadn't left footprints that time. It turned to the side, pointed, and then moved out of the way. Billy and I didn't need to be told twice and we both ran in the direction it was pointing in. We somehow knew, without a word being spoken, that the creature or whatever it was had just pointed us in the right direction out of the woods. We ran for almost a half hour, and it was scary because we never even realized how deep in the forest we had ended up. Billy stopped short once we got to his yard though. All over the cabin and surrounding it, on the rooftop and all over the yard, were shadow beings of all types, shapes, and sizes. Some of them were animals and some looked like the shapes of unknown creatures we hadn't ever seen before. These ones left footprints. We were terrified but one by one they disappeared. Except for the ones on the roof. We knew we hadn't been hallucinating either because they left behind all different kinds of footprints, including the hooves and skinny feet we had seen earlier. We were reluctant to run closer though because the shadows on the roof were jumping from the rooftop to nearby trees and then onto the roof of the garage and back again. There were five of them and they all looked different. They exuded evil and we knew they were demonic even though I don't think we really knew what that even meant at the time. We could see the light shining from the huge, sliding glass doors that led to the deck and as we inched closer through the yard, we saw his mother standing in the kitchen. She was on the phone and suddenly there was a large and very terrifying shadow being behind her. She must've felt it because she suddenly jumped and turned around. It was like she didn't see it and turned back around to continue the conversation she was having with whoever it was on the other end of the line.

Finally, we just decided once again to take our chances and ran. Just as we were about to reach the door Billy's father came out of it. He yelled at us for being late and making his mother worry. She was just about to call the police, he said. He was angry but could tell we were terrified, so his voice softened as he ushered us inside. He looked up at the roof but didn't react and it was as though he too couldn't see the entities on top of it, leaping around like it was their only job. We were sent to bed immediately after eating as a sort of punishment for not being home on time and being so late once we did finally get there. His father wouldn't let us explain but even if he did what would we have said? He never would have believed us and was a real no nonsense type of man. We laid down but the excitement we had always felt during sleepovers at the cabin was gone. We both knew the place was evil but wondered why we hadn't ever seen anything before. I still don't have the answer to that question or so many more I bet you want to ask me. I fell asleep after Billy did because I was the one who was more scared of the dark and the events of that night didn't help that any, not at all. I remember waking up in the middle of the night and having to walk downstairs to get to the bathroom. I sat up and just as I was about to step out of the bed, I saw a shadow person leaning casually against the bedroom door on the inside. It had a fedora style hat on and glowing red eyes. It growled at me, and I stayed in the bed, shivering and shaking with fear and terror for another hour as it inched closer and close to the bed before finally making its way over to the closet and disappearing into it. I ran to the bathroom and back again and told Billy about it the next day. We never stopped seeing the shadow entities, but we never talked about it either. We continued visiting the cabin well into our adulthoods and every single year we would hope and pray that we didn't have any visitations but every year we would be disappointed. While no one ever died in the house, it seems like each year someone else who had been there got very sick or had some sort of strange and uncanny accident. We knew the house itself was evil and we could see the evil entities inside of it. The cabin still stands, and Billy owns it and still visits every year, but he's never brought his family there and in fact I'm not sure his wife even knows the place exists. Same with me, I will visit with him sometimes, but I never bring my family. I never have and I never will. I am afraid that someone is going to get possessed by or killed because of the entities but it hasn't happened yet. The more I research shadow beings, and there's plenty of research out there online nowadays, the more I feel like they are just waiting for the right time to enact their evil plan. Whatever that may be, I'm sure I don't know.

TWELVE

HELLHOUND

BACK IN THE early 90s I took my young son camping in the Appalachian Mountains near where we live on the east coast. He was five years old at the time and we were both excited because his mother had been saying all along that once he started kindergarten then he would finally be able to go camping with me. Our house has a lot of woods that surround it, so I was always taking him fishing and hiking or simply walking through the woods and playing with him. We would go on picnics together, sometimes all of us as a family, and even go into the woods a little way to walk our dogs at night. There was no fear of the woods by my son, and I knew that over the spring vacation would be a great time to take him out to go camping. It was going to be a "guy's weekend" with just me and my son and I couldn't get out the door fast enough. We didn't have cell phones back then and I knew his mother was a nervous wreck, but we only planned on being gone for three nights and I had been an avid camper and outdoorsman ever since I was my son's age at that time. My dad started taking me on trips into the wilderness when I was five years old. Growing up with my father I also learned how to be a very good hunter as well, but my values changed as I got older and there came a time right after high school that I no longer was comfortable killing an animal for no other reason than sport. I wouldn't be teaching my son how to hunt but I did always carry a gun with me into the woods just in case. It was especially important to me at that time because my skin was so small and inexperienced in the woods and with camping. He knew not to wander off with anyone though and so for the most part, aside from wild animals, I wasn't too worried about anything scaring him out there. I had no idea that the most terrifying thing in both of our lives would happen during that camping trip.

We arrived at the campgrounds at around five at night and I checked us in. We then hiked out to the spot where we would be spending all three of our nights. It struck me as odd right away that there were hardly any other people camping there. The weather was beautiful and was very mild and perfect for being outdoors and a lot of public schools in the area, if not all of them, were on spring break at the time. My son was so excited, and he talked to me about it the entire three-hour drive there. We laughed and had a lot of fun, but I noticed his demeanor changed to one of nervousness and confusion almost as soon as we started hiking through the woods to our spot. I asked him repeatedly what was wrong, but he kept trying to reassure me that he was just excited and a little bit scared about being in "such big woods" as he put it. Remember he was five years old and perfectly capable of accurately naming his emotions and I didn't have any reason to believe that something else was going on with him based on his demeanor the whole ride there. I figured once we got settled in and I got the camp set up, he would become more comfortable and calm down a bit. I brought along an extra tent in case he wanted to stay by himself, and I set that one up right next to mine which was an extra-large one that would easily fit the both of us and probably two more average sized adults. I took camping very seriously and walked my son through all the preparations and set up step by step. He seemed very interested and insisted on helping me with every- thing which made me happy. We ate by the fire and afterwards roasted marshmallows. We talked about everything under the sun for about an hour after that and around ten o'clock he was finally tired enough to go to sleep. He said he wanted to try to sleep in the extra tent. I think he wanted to be a "big boy" and so I let him but told him I would be right next to him so if at any time he got scared for any reason or otherwise wanted or needed to come into mine, that would be perfectly fine. He still seemed a little jittery, but he was doing a lot better than he had been when we first got there, and I didn't want to press the issue because his mind seems to have moved on from whatever it was that had been bothering him.

I showed my son where to go when he got up in the middle of the night to go to the bathroom and explained why we can't just go anywhere, especially not right there in our camp. I told him to feel free to wake me up when that happens so that I could go with him because I figured he would be a little scared maybe. The woods when you're that far deep in them and it's the first time, can be a little intimidating. He said he would be okay, and I figured he would too. After all, he was big enough to know when to wake me up and I had only seen a handful of other campers along the way out there and none of them were even close to how far I took him out. I didn't want to have to deal with any weirdos or troublemakers while I was out there trying to spend some quality time with my son. We said our goodnights and went to sleep. I thought I heard him whispering in the middle of the night. I was half asleep when I first heard what sounded like him whispering in a full-blown conversation with another voice that sounded strange to me but before I could really put my finger on it, I must've fallen back asleep. I asked him about it the next morning, but he denied ever waking up at all, let alone having a full-blown conversation with a stranger. I believed him because I didn't have any reason not to and we went on with our day. We did everything we had on our list of things to do. We went fishing, we hiked up the side of one of the little mountains, we played hide and seek, and we went swimming in some man-made water areas nearby to where our camp was. It was a really great day but there was this overwhelming sense of being watched that kept getting to me. I was looking all around and trying to see if someone was following us, but I never did see anyone. I couldn't shake the feeling but decided to just be extra diligent without telling my son why. We stopped for lunch and while we were eating, I kept seeing him looking behind me, as though he were staring at, and his eyes were following something. I thought maybe he had spotted some sort of animal but when I turned around and didn't see anything or anyone where he had been looking, I asked him about it, but he simply said he hadn't been staring at anything. Once again, I didn't want him to think that I was calling him a liar, he was a very sensitive and honest little boy, and I let it go. We eventually made our way back to the camp and got ready for bed. It was on that second night that everything would change.

Everything was fine and perfectly normal until I woke up once again in the middle of the night to my five-year-old whispering and there seemed to be someone responding. As if that weren't troubling enough, I couldn't understand what either of them were saying but the other person's voice sounded very deep, like they were growling and very distorted. I would say it even sounded demonic, like how they make the voices of demon's sound in movies, and I remember even thinking that's what it sounded like back then. I started to immediately fall back asleep again and really had to fight to stay awake. I must've fallen asleep again for like a minute, but it was like being stuck in a state of sleep paralysis where I was fighting to stay awake with everything that I had, and my adrenaline was pumping. I knew there was someone at my son's tent, which was right next to mine, but if I didn't wake up or if I wasn't able to start moving, I wouldn't know who it was, and they could end up leaving the forest with him. All these terrible thoughts were running through my mind and every time I would try to force my eyes to stay open, I would see dark shadows flying around all over my tent and seeming like they were sort of bouncing off all the sides of it. Finally, I sat straight up and even though my adrenaline was pumping, I was still in an extreme state of hyper awareness and knew I had to protect my son at all costs. I didn't want the other person running off with my son though or being spooked and leaving altogether without me being able to see and confront them, so I just sat there regaining my composure, slowing my heart rate, and listening intently to try and hear what was happening right next to me in my son's tent. I still could hear them talking and then I heard my son start to move around and the zipper on his tent was zipped open. I knew it had been closed because I had zipped it for him before we went to bed. I looked at my watch and it was a little after three o'clock in the morning. I planned on jumping out of my tent and surprising the perpetrator and possibly taking him to the ground before figuring out what to do with him, but I wanted to see what was happening first and if he was trying to take my son somewhere. I couldn't believe what I saw.

I saw my son walking into the woods, near where I had told him he needed to go if he had to use the bathroom. But at first, I didn't see anything or anyone else. I looked closer and that's when I saw a gigantic shadow on the ground and on the one side of his tent. His flashlight was on inside of the tent and the way the moon was illuminating the whole camping area it was perfect for me to have been able to clearly see that shadow. I looked from the giant shadow back to my son and there was suddenly a figure behind him. It was a gigantic dog. It was walking on all fours but was taller than my son anyway. The head and jaws were bigger than two of my heads combined and like two of the biggest Rottweilers you ever saw. It was unimaginably and indescribably huge. I don't even know how else to explain it. It did look like a Rottweiler.

I yelled out to my son, and he immediately stopped walking and turned around, but he looked like he was in some sort of daze or trance and like he was looking right through me. I yelled for him to come to me, and he blinked and snapped out of it completely. He stood there and immediately started to cry and then came running around the creature and into my arms. I told him to get into my tent and don't come out no matter what. He did so but I knew that he was watching the whole thing.

I stood there and was ready to take the dog beast on if I had to. It turned around and stood on its hind legs. So, it was standing on two legs, like a human being. It was at least thirteen feet tall and eight feet wide. It had strange hands. They weren't paws but they weren't human either and were more like some sick and twisted version of both those things put together. Its feet were gigantic dog paws, or so they seemed from where I was standing. Its eyes were blazing red and almost looked like there was a literal fire in them. It was like looking at a film or something of a fire, but I could see it in the thing's eyes. It growled at me, and I could see thick slobber and drool dripping down its chin and onto the dirt below where it was standing. Then, the distorted voice started invading my head and even though I couldn't understand what it was saying, I was starting to feel weak and dizzy. I was going to pass out and that's exactly what the beast wanted. I started reciting some prayers I learned back in Sunday school from my youth. I wasn't a religious person at that time, but I had to do something and something deep inside of me, or perhaps it was another voice but that one was more dominating in my head than the demonic one, was imploring me to pray any prayers that I knew and not to stop and so that's what I did.

The dog beast let out a loud howl and then it screeched like it was in pain, but it didn't sound like an animal then, it sounded like a human being screaming in pain. Then, within the blink of an eye, a gigantic dark shadow appeared and shot off into the woods. All the little black shadows that had been darting around my tent earlier, which I had completely forgotten about when I sent my son in there thinking he would be safe, came darting out of my tent and followed it off into the wilderness.

I got back inside of the tent with my son and though he was terrified and obviously had been traumatized by the entire ordeal, he was asleep within seconds and for that I was grateful. I stayed up all night and the next morning packed us up to leave. The strangest part of all was that my son had no memory of anything that had happened the night before. He didn't understand why we were leaving, and he had no fears at all about staying another night. He thought he had just crawled into my tent with me after getting up and going to the bathroom. I saw no reason to terrify or traumatize him all over again so I just told him I wasn't feeling well and that I would make it up to him with another trip. He was okay with that, and we went home. I told my wife the same story I told my son, and she also took me at my word.

My son gushed to her about how much fun we had but I was distracted and wanted answers so on my way to work a few days later I went to the library and found out that what we experienced out there was a hellhound. If you don't know what they are I suggest you look them up. It's terrifying to think something like that was not only visiting but trying to take off into the woods with my little boy. The thought sickens me even now, all these years later. We never had another experience with a hellhound or any other paranormal or supernatural crea-ture. We went back to church and had many amazing camping trips or trips into the woods in general since then and it's still something my son and I do today. Nowadays we bring his kids with us and sometimes the whole family comes along. We were very fortunate and to whatever being helped me out that night, whatever force helped me fight passing out and almost forced me to start praying, I will be forever grateful. I think for sure it was a guardian angel.

THIRTEEN

FOREST DEMON

WHEN PEOPLE THINK of New Jersey, they usually think of industrial areas, big cities, diners, and New York but so many of them forget that New Jersey is called the Garden State and it's called that for a reason. We gained a bad reputation and have come to be known as the garbage state because people who fly into Newark airport to go to New York City only get to see one small area along the highway, on the way to New York City, that's full of shipping docks and factories. It's quite beautiful here if you know where to go. I have lived here all my life and raised my kids here. In fact, my whole family for three generations before me have been from New Jersey and the ones before that came over on a ship from Ireland. I know a lot about Irish legends and folklore, and I learned most of it from my grandmother. She would tell me stories for hours on end about all the spirits of the forests and how to appease them so when I was in the woods, I didn't get myself into trouble or attacked by them. I grew up listening to that type of stuff and by the time I was eighteen years old, which is when my encounter happened, I was well prepared for anything that I happened to come across out there in the wilderness, whether it be natural or supernatural in nature. I have always lived in northern New Jersey which is more urban and has more of a city feel to it in most of the towns but when I turned eighteen, I wanted to be independent and the only good rental I could find was about two hours south from where I grew up and would technically be considered southern New Jersey. It was a bit of a bummer because I didn't want to leave behind my family and all my friends, but we all had our own vehicles and would end up seeing each other often anyway. My encounter happened right after I moved into my own apartment. I had just spent a week unpacking boxes and getting everything arranged exactly how I wanted it, and I desperately needed a break. The house I was renting was a tiny little one bedroom, but it was big enough for me and it was on a horse farm. The owners of the farm immediately took me under their wing and befriended me. They were an old married couple without any children, and they were delighted that I was going to be renting from them. I had always been an animal lover, but I had been the only one like that in my family, so I never got to have pets or anything like that. I was thrilled to be around the horses and all the other animals and would help every spare second of my day. That's how this all started.

I had been helping feed and brush the horses when the man I was renting from asked me if I had the chance to explore the woods yet. He meant the deep and dense wilderness that surrounded the entire property for miles and miles in every direction. I told him that I hadn't, and he said that I was missing out and if I liked to walk in the woods, that was exactly the right place for me. I told him I would check it out and left it at that. I went back home and took a shower, but I couldn't stop looking out my windows. It was a gorgeous and very mild day and eventually I decided to go for a walk in the woods to just get some fresh air and relax a bit. The elderly couple I was renting from had mentioned at some point to me that they had places antique benches all throughout the trails as far as their property went, which was several hundred acres at that time, and that they often went for strolls out there to upkeep some of the forest and make sure it was suitable for when they wanted to go out there and read or have picnics in one of the many clearings. I had the bright idea to grab a book and head out into the forest to sit on one of the benches and read. I hadn't done that in so long and where I come from the only forest, I would see would be more than two trees together in the same place. There wasn't anything left of mother nature in the crowded and overpopulated town I spent most of my childhood in. It seemed like a good idea at the time, and I was excited. I packed a little snack for myself, grabbed a water and a book, and headed out into the woods.

I had to walk quite a distance to get through the entire property that made up the farm and to the trails in the woods, but I eventually made it. I walked for a little while, but I immediately had a very strange feeling from the moment I entered it. I know many people describe things like this when telling others about their own encounters out in the forest but it's true. It was like the peace was drained right out of me and I was suddenly on high alert and somewhat frightened. There didn't seem to be any good reason for it and so I kept on going. I was looking for one of the many benches the couple said they had personally placed out there. It dawned on me after a few moments as to why I was feeling the way I was and that's because it was broad daylight on a beautiful and mild summer day and yet it was so quiet out there you would literally have been able to hear a pin drop. I tried to just shake it off and not pay too much attention to it but even with as unfamiliar with the forest as I was, I knew there had to have been a reason for it and whatever that reason was, it couldn't have been good. I wanted so badly to enjoy the peace and quiet of the forest though that I kept pushing it out of my mind. Finally, after about forty-five minutes of walking along several trails in the eerily quiet forest, I came to one of the benches. I hadn't realized they were so deep in the forest but once I made it to that first one, I was happy that it was further away from the farm. It made me feel like I was in a fairytale all my own and I was starting to feel comfortable and happy again. I had heard a few birds chirping just then so I figured I had been overreacting to how quiet the place was, but I would have done anything to convince myself of that so I didn't have to face the fact that I might have been putting myself in some sort of danger by being out there. I sat and read for about twenty minutes before the silence of the forest was shaken abruptly by what sounded like something clawing at something else. It sounded like a cat scratching its post, I guess is a good way to put it.

I knew enough to know there were no cats out there in the middle of the woods and I hadn't even seen any other animals out there, not even your average squirrel and even though I heard a few bird chirps, I hadn't been able to locate any of those either. I stopped and looked around, trying to find the source of the noises I was hearing. They sounded very out of place to me, but I wasn't sure if that was because of how quiet it had been all along up until that point or if the noises just didn't belong in the middle of the woods. Maybe, I told myself, it was a little bit of both. I didn't see anything at first and decided to just go back to reading my book, but the noise was very grating on my ears and distracting so I got up and went to look around a little more. I stopped short on the trail I had been walking when I first saw it. It took a moment for my eyes to adjust but even then, I couldn't easily tell what I was looking at. It sorts of looked like a dog riding a horse or something, but I blinked and looked again, and the shape had changed a little bit. Whatever it was, it was facing away from me and scratching its nails down a nearby tree. It was like a cat scratching a post after all, but this was no cat. The figure, or whatever it was- at that point I had no clue what I could have been looking at- stopped scratching and started walking along the same trail that I was walking on, but its back was still turned to me, and it was walking in the same direction that I was facing. I tried not to make a sound as I decided what to do next. I didn't want to follow it, but I didn't want to turn my back on it either. I didn't know what to do but the choice stopped being my own when I heard a woman's voice whispering through the trees and that had been carried to me along the wind. It told me to, "follow." That's it. It only said one word and it was almost like I couldn't resist it. Well, at least that's what I told myself. I started slowly walking behind it, still trying to not make any noise to alert it to my presence despite my knowing it had already spotted me. I felt confused but within about a minute or two my mind cleared, and I realized what I was doing. I stopped short and was planning on turning around and running when the figure walking in front of me turned around too. That's when I finally got to see what it was.

It was about ten feet tall and wore a long black robe with the hood up over the back of its head. Its hair, which I could only see a little bit of in the front, was very white. There were what looked like antlers coming up out of each side of its head, just like you would see on a fully mature buck, but it was made of tree branches. It was definitely a part of the physical makeup of whatever this creature was and not some handmade horns or anything like that. It had small black dots all over its nose and under its eyes, like freckles, but they were much larger than any freckles I had ever seen on any human being's face. Its eyes are what stood out to me the most though. Where we have whites, it had red and where we have color, its eyes were green. They were slanted upwards and even though the skin was deathly pale, the creature somehow looked beautiful to me. At least, the part I've described to you so far was beautiful. Its cape fell off it and I'm not sure if that was magic or what, but it fell to the ground. The thing had leaves covering "her" breasts and a flat stomach that looked very human, aside from being very pale. It was very slim and well-toned. It seemed like it had the perfect body without a single flaw at all, that is, until I saw the hands and feet. The feet were cloven hooves and the hands ended in what I can only describe as talons. It took me about three minutes of standing their face to face and just about ten feet away from this thing before it finally moved. It's almost like it wanted me to see all of it before it did what it did next. It seemed very calculated and even now looking back on it that's exactly what it seems like still. It quickly got down on all fours. Its hind side was much higher than its front side. It suddenly was growling at me like an animal and slobbering all over the ground and its own chin. Its teeth were black and rotting out of its mouth and the second this happened, the stench of rot and decay overpowered everything, and I felt like I was about to vomit right there on the spot. It put its head in such a way that I knew it was about to charge at me if I didn't do something, but I was so terrified and shocked that I really couldn't move. I turned and ran.

The entity ran after me, but it was incredibly slow because of how it had to run while on all fours. It seemed to me like it would have been so much faster had it just run on its hind legs but who knows? I made it to the farm, and I was screaming for help. The elderly couple came running to me and as I tried explaining to them what I had just encountered, they gave one another a knowing look and asked me if I would join them for some tea. I said okay, and once I calmed down and was able to tell them the whole story, they told me that they had seen that thing over a dozen times in the fifty years they had been living there and every time they did, they lost a horse that same night. It would be found the next morning, ripped apart and inside out. I don't want to get too graphic, so I'll leave it at that. I lived there another five years and eventually moved on once I got married and started my family, but I visited often and eventually, after they passed, I bought the farm and the house that went with it. I have only ever seen it one other time. I've done my research and I think it was one of the forest nymphs or a different sort of forest demon that my grandma used to warn me about when I was a little girl. Needless to say, no one in my family, including myself, ever goes into those woods alone and no one ever goes out there at all at nighttime. Oh, and by the way, the elderly couple did lose a horse

that very next day, just the way they said they were
going to.

————

CONTINUE WITH
MYSTERIES IN THE DARK, VOLUME 2

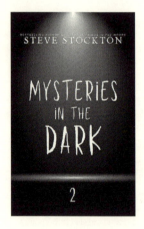

ABOUT THE AUTHOR

Steve Stockton is a veteran outdoorsman and author who has been investigating the unexplained for over 35 years. Originally from the mountains of East Tennessee, Steve has traveled all over the country and many parts of the world and now makes his home in picturesque New England with his wife, Nicole, and their dog, Mulder.

Steve cites his influences as his "gypsy witch" grandmother, who told him multitudes of legends and stories as a small child, as well as authors such as Frank Edwards, John Keel, Charles Fort, Loren Coleman, Ivan Sanderson, Colin Wilson, and Nick Redfern.

His published books include Strange Things in the Woods (a collection of true, paranormal encounters) as well as the autobiographical My Strange World, where he talks about his own experiences dating back to childhood. Recently, he has written National Park Mysteries and Disappearances, Volumes 1, 2, and 3.

He also owns and narrates the wildly popular Among The Missing Youtube channel.

MYSTERIES IN THE DARK

STRANGE THINGS IN THE WOODS

NATIONAL PARK MYSTERIES & DISAPPEARANCES

MY STRANGE WORLD

13 PAST MIDNIGHT

ALSO BY FREE REIGN PUBLISHING

ENCOUNTERS IN THE WOODS

WHAT LURKS BEYOND

FEAR IN THE FOREST

INTO THE DARKNESS

ENCOUNTERS BIGFOOT

TALES OF TERROR

I SAW BIGFOOT

STALKED: TERRIFYING TRUE CRIME STORIES

MYSTERIES IN THE DARK

13 PAST MIDNIGHT

THINGS IN THE WOODS

CONSPIRACY THEORIES THAT WERE TRUE

LOVE ENCOUNTERS

STAT: CRAZY MEDICAL STORIES

CRASH: STORIES FROM THE EMERGENCY ROOM

LEGENDS AND STORIES: FROM THE APPALACHIAN
TRAIL

Made in United States
Orlando, FL
16 September 2024

51550574R00100